Michael M. Dediu

Vergilius, Horatius Ovidius, and Shakespeare

A chronological and photographic documentary

DERC Publishing House
Tewksbury (Boston), Massachusetts, U. S. A.

Published and printed in the
United States of America
On the Great Seal of the United States are included:
E Pluribus Unum (Out of many, one)
Annuit Coeptis (He has approved of the undertakings)
Novus Ordo Seclorum (New order of the ages)

Library of Congress Control Number: 2018902980

Dediu, Michael M.

Vergilius, Horatius, Ovidius, and Shakespeare
A chronological and photographic documentary

ISBN-13: 978-1-939757654

Preface

Who said "*A home without books is a body without soul*"?

You guessed it – it was Marcus Tullius Cicero (3 Jan 106 BC – 7 Dec 43 BC, aged 63.9), more than 2050 years ago. When Cicero died, Vergilius was 27, Horatius 22, and Ovidius just over 8.5 months, therefore Cicero probably had some of the great poems of Vergilius and Horatius.

A quote of Vergilius is "*Felix, qui potuit rerum cognoscere causas*" - Fortunate is he, who understood the causes of things. Hundreds of generations of students learned from Vergilius' Aeneid, as it profoundly changed how the Romans, and then all the world, think about poetry.

Horatius said "*Aequam memento rebus in arduis servare mentem*" - Remember to maintain a calm mind while doing difficult tasks. He certainly maintain a calm mind, and his poetry themes, like the beatus ille (an appraisal of simple life), and carpe diem ("enjoy the day") gained more and more importance to this day.

Ovidius: "*Omnia mutantur, nihil interit*" - All things change, nothing perishes. He is best known for his 15-book epic narrative poem Metamorphoses, which changed everything.

Shakespeare "*Brevity is the soul of wit.*" He is the best-selling fiction author of all time (estimated 4 billions of copies sold).

The lives of these legendary authors are fascinating, and this book for the general public is focused on a variety of relevant information not only about them, but also about numerous other personalities (Pythagoras, Plato, Cicero, Caesar, Antonius, Augustus) and important events. There are also many attractive photographs, and I thank my wife Sophia for her photo assistance.

The more you read, the more you'll love it!

On 27 March 1912 my father Vergiliu Dediu was born – he was a good electrical engineer, and a very good father and grandfather (his grandsons are Horatiu and Ovidiu….). We celebrate his 106th birthday, and I dedicate this book to his memory.

Michael M. Dediu, Ph. D.

Tewksbury (Boston), U. S. A., 26 March 2018

Michael M. Dediu is also the author of these books (which can be found on Amazon.com):

1. Aphorisms and quotations – with examples and explanations
2. Axioms, aphorisms and quotations – with examples and explanations
3. 100 Great Personalities and their Quotations
4. Professor Petre P. Teodorescu – A Great Mathematician and Engineer
5. Professor Ioan Goia – A Dedicated Engineering Professor
6. Venice (Venezia) – a new perspective. A short presentation with photographs
7. La Serenissima (Venice) - a new photographic perspective. A short presentation with many photos
8. Grand Canal – Venice. A new photographic viewpoint. A short presentation with many photos
9. Piazza San Marco – Venice. A different photographic view. A short presentation with many photos
10. Roma (Rome) - La Città Eterna. A new photographic view. A short presentation with many photos
11. Why is Rome so Fascinating? A short presentation with many photos
12. Rome, Boston and Helsinki. A short photographic presentation
13. Rome and Tokyo – two captivating cities. A short photographic presentation
14. Beautiful Places on Earth – A new photographic presentation
15. From Niagara Falls to Mount Fuji via Rome - A novel photographic presentation
16. From the USA and Canada to Italy and Japan - A fresh photographic presentation
17. Paris – Why So Many Call This City Mon Amour - A lovely photographic presentation
18. The City of Light – Paris (La Ville-Lumière) - A kaleidoscopic photographic presentation
19. Paris (Lutetia Parisiorum) – the romance capital of the world - A kaleidoscopic photographic view
20. Paris and Tokyo – a joyful photographic presentation. With a preamble about the Universe

21. From USA to Japan via Canada – A cheerful photographic documentary
22. 200 Wonderful Places, In The Last 50 Years – A personal photographic documentary
23. Must see places in USA and Japan - A kaleidoscopic photographic documentary
24. Grandeurs of the World - A kaleidoscopic photographic documentary
25. Corneliu Leu – writer on the same wavelength as Mark Twain. An American viewpoint
26. From Berkeley to Pompeii via Rome – A kaleidoscopic photographic documentary
27. From America to Europe via Japan - A kaleidoscopic photographic documentary
28. Discover America and Japan - A photographic documentary
29. J. R. Lucas – philosopher on a creative parallel with Plato, An American viewpoint
30. From America to Switzerland via France - A photographic documentary
31. From Bretton Woods to New York via Cape Cod - A photographic documentary
32. Splendid Places on the Atlantic Coast of the U. S. A. - A photographic documentary
33. Fourteen nice Cities on three Continents - A photographic documentary
34. 17 Picturesque Cities on the World Map - A photographic documentary
35. Unforgettable Places from Four Continents including Trump buildings - A photographic documentary
36. Dediu Newsletter, Volume 1, Number 1, 6 December 2016 – Monthly news, review, comments and suggestions for a better and wiser world
37. Dediu Newsletter, Volume 1, Number 2, 6 January 2017 (available at www.derc.com).
38. Dediu Newsletter, Volume 1, Number 3, 6 February 2017 (available at www.derc.com).
39. London and Greenwich, A photographic documentary
40. Dediu Newsletter, Volume 1, Number 4, 6 March 2017 (available also at www.derc.com).

41. Dediu Newsletter, Volume 1, Number 5, 6 April 2017 (available also at www.derc.com).
42. Dediu Newsletter, Volume 1, Number 6, 6 May 2017 (available also at www.derc.com).
43. Dediu Newsletter, Volume 1, Number 7, 6 June 2017 (available also at www.derc.com).
44. London, Oxford and Cambridge, A photographic documentary
45. Dediu Newsletter, Volume 1, Number 8, 6 July 2017 (available also at www.derc.com).
46. Dediu Newsletter, Volume 1, Number 9, 6 August 2017 (available also at www.derc.com).
47. Dediu Newsletter, Volume 1, Number 10, 6 September 2017 (available also at www.derc.com).
48. Three Great Professors: President Woodrow Wilson, Historian Germán Arciniegas, Mathematician Gheorghe Vrănceanu, A chronological and photographic documentary
49. Dediu Newsletter, Volume 1, Number 11, 6 October 2017 (available also at www.derc.com).
50. Dediu Newsletter, Volume 1, Number 12, 6 November 2017 (available also at www.derc.com).
51. Dediu Newsletter, Volume 2, Number 1 (13), 6 December 2017 (available also at www.derc.com).
52. Two Great Leaders: Augustus and George Washington, A chronological and photographic documentary
53. Dediu Newsletter, Volume 2, Number 2 (14), 6 January 2018 (available also at www.derc.com).
54. Newton, Benjamin Franklin, and Gauss, A chronological and photographic documentary
55. Dediu Newsletter, Volume 2, Number 3 (15), 6 February 2018 (available also at www.derc.com).
56. 2017: World Top Events, But Many Little Known, A chronological and photographic documentary
57. Dediu Newsletter, Volume 2, Number 4 (16), 6 March 2018 (available also at www.derc.com).

Michael M. Dediu is the editor of these books (also on Amazon.com):

1. Sophia Dediu: The life and its torrents – Ana. In Europe around 1920
2. Proceedings of the 4th International Conference "Advanced Composite Materials Engineering" COMAT 2012
3. Adolf Shvedchikov: I am an eternal child of spring – poems in English, Italian, French, German, Spanish and Russian
4. Adolf Shvedchikov: Life's Enigma – poems in English, Italian and Russian
5. Adolf Shvedchikov: Everyone wants to be HAPPY – poems in English, Spanish and Russian
6. Adolf Shvedchikov: My Life, My Love – poems in English, Italian and Russian
7. Adolf Shvedchikov: I am the gardener of love – poems in English and Russian
8. Adolf Shvedchikov: Amaretta di Saronno – poems in English and Russian
9. Adolf Shvedchikov: A Russian Rediscovers America
10. Adolf Shvedchikov: Parade of Life - poems in English and Russian
11. Adolf Shvedchikov: Overcoming Sorrow - poems in English and Russian
12. Sophia Dediu: Sophia meets Japan
13. Corneliu Leu: Roosevelt, Churchill, Stalin and Hitler: Their surprising role in Eastern Europe in 1944
14. Proceedings of the 5th International Conference "Computational Mechanics and Virtual Engineering" COMEC 2013
15. Georgeta Simion – Potanga: Beyond Imagination: A Thought-provoking novel inspired from mid-20th century events
16. Ana Dediu: The poetry of my life in Europe and The USA
17. Ana Dediu: The Four Graces
18. Proceedings of the 5th International Conference "Advanced Composite Materials Engineering" COMAT 2014
19. Sophia Dediu: Chocolate Cook Book: Is there such a thing as too much chocolate?

20. Sorin Vlase: Mechanical Identifiability in Automotive Engineering
21. Gabriel Dima: The Evolution of the Aerostructures – Concept and Technologies
22. Proceedings of the 6th International Conference "Computational Mechanics and Virtual Engineering" COMEC 2015
23. Sophia Dediu: Cook Book 1 A-B-C Common sense cooking
24. Sophia Dediu: Dim Sum Spring Festival
25. Ana Dediu & Sophia Dediu: Europe in 1985 - A chronological and photographic documentary

Table of Contents

Chapter 1. Vergilius and Horatius

70 BC – 15 October - Publius Vergilius Maro was born in the farming village of Andes (now Virgilio), 6 km south of the city of Mantova (now Mantua, in Lombardia), 130 km southeast of Milano, in the Roman Republic province of Gallia Cisalpina, in northern Italy, to a wealthy equestrian farming family. Vergilius was raised on his family's farm, and the Italian countryside, with its people, which influenced him early on, and was later echoed through his poetry.

Gnaeus Pompeius Magnus (29 Sep 106 BC – 28 Sep 48 BC, aged 57 years 11 months and 29 days (1 day short of 58)), also known in English as Pompey or Pompey the Great, a military and political leader of the late Roman Republic), now 36, and Marcus Licinius Crassus (115 BC – 53 BC, aged 62, a Roman general and politician who played a key role in the transformation of the Roman Republic into the Roman Empire), now 45, started their first consulship.

69 BC – Cleopatra VII Philopator was born (69 BC – 12 August 30 BC, aged 39).

Octavia Minor, or the Young, or Octavia, the elder sister of the future first Roman Emperor, Augustus, was born (69 BC – 11 BC, aged 58).

65 BC – 8 December – Quintus Horatius Flaccus was born, in Venusia (City of Venus, now Venosa, elevation 415 m, in the province of Potenza, 130 km east of Napoli, 300 km southeast of Rome, 620 km southeast of Andes (now Virgilio)), a small town between the border regions of Apulia and Lucania (Basilicata, the Vulture area), in the Samnite (south of Italy) in the Roman Republic. Images of his childhood setting, and references to it, are found throughout his poems.

His father was a slave, and then a Roman freedman, and owned a small farm in Venusia. Later he moved to Rome, where he worked as a coactor, middleman between buyers and sellers at auctions, receiving 1% of the purchase price. Horatius' father spend very much money on Horatius' education, and sent him to the best school in Rome, the Grammaticus Orbilius (Lucius Orbilius Pupillus (114 BC – 14 BC, aged 100) was a Latin grammarian of the 1st century BC, who taught at school, first at Benevento and then at Rome, where Horatius, around 10 years old, was his pupil, Orbilius being around 59). Later Horatius was sent by his father to Athens to study Greek and philosophy. Horatius was always very grateful to his father.

Vergilius was 5 years, 1 month and 23 days.

63 BC – Cicero, 43, is consul. Marcus Tullius Cicero (3 Jan 106 BC – 7 Dec 43 BC, aged 63.9) was a Roman politician and orator, who served as consul in the year 63 BC. He came from a wealthy municipal family of the Roman equestrian order, and is considered one of Rome's greatest orators and prose stylists.

23 September – Gaius Octavius, later Augustus, was born, when Vergilius was almost 7, and Horatius almost 2. Octavius was raised by his grandmother, Julia Minor, 42, the older sister of Julius Caesar, now 37 (Gaius Julius Caesar (13 July 100 BC – 15 March 44 BC, aged 55.6), usually called Julius Caesar, was a Roman politician and general who played a critical role in the events that led to the passing of the Roman Republic and the rise of the Roman Empire).

60 BC – Vergilius, 10, was sent by his father to study at Cremona (60 km west of Andes (now Virgilio), 75 km southeast of Milano, north of river Po, in Lombardia, where Antonio Stradivari (1644 – 1737, aged 93) will craft for 81 years (from the age of 12 to 93) the best over 700 violins, cellos, guitars and harps, cold Stradivarius).

The first triumvirate started - a political alliance between three powerful men in the Roman Republic: Gaius Julius Caesar (40), Marcus Licinius Crassus (55), and Gnaeus Pompeius Magnus (46). It was formed in 60 BC, and lasted until 53 BC.

57 BC – Vergilius, 13, was moved by his father to study at Mediolanum (now Milano, founded around 600 BC, and in 222 BC the Romans renamed it Mediolanum).

59 BC – Caesar, 41, starts his first consulship.

58 BC – Caesar, 42, was in Gaul (now France) for 9 years, until 49 BC.

55 BC– Pompeius, 51, and Crassus, 60, started their second consulship.

53 BC – Vergilius, 17, was moved by his father to Rome to continue his studies in rhetoric, medicine, astronomy, philosophy, and law.

Marcus Licinius Crassus died (115 BC – 53 BC, aged 62, a Roman general and politician who played a key role in the transformation of the Roman Republic into the Roman Empire).

The first triumvirate ends.

Italy, Rome, Forum Caesaris (46 BC, by Julius Caesar (100 – 44 BC), 160 m by 75 m, with Temple of Venus Genetrix (down)), Via dei Fori Imperiali (center left), Forum Augustus (left, 2 BC), Amphitheatrum Flavium (right up, 80, wrongly called Colosseum).

51 BC: Julia Minor, 54, the grandmother (from the mother side) of Octavius (now 12 years old), and older sister of Julius Caesar (49), dies. At her funeral Octavius delivers the eulogy, which is his first public appearance, and impresses his great-uncle Julius Caesar, 49.

49 BC– Julius Caesar, 51, returns from Gaul, and crosses the river Rubicon (in northeastern Italy, south of Ravenna), entering Roman Republic, and soon he seizes control of Rome.

Soon after, Vergilius, 21, moved to Napoli (Naples), and studies with Greek (perhaps Epicurean) scholars there.

Italy, 3 Nov 2009, Cividale del Friuli (founded by Julius Caesar (100 BC – 44 BC) in 50 BC with the name of Forum Iulii, 15 km east of Udine, 135 m, in the foothills of the eastern Alps, population 12,000), Piazza Foro Giulio Cesare, with nice trees.

48 BC: 28 Sep - Gnaeus Pompeius Magnus died (29 Sep 106 BC – 28 Sep 48 BC, aged 57 years 11 months and 29 days (1 day short of 58)), also known in English as Pompey or Pompey the Great, a military and political leader of the late Roman Republic).

On 18 October Octavius, 15, donned toga virilis, and was elected to the Pontifical College.

46 BC– Horatius, 19, left Rome, and continued his formal education in Athens, a great center of learning in the ancient world, enrolling in The Academy (founded in 385 BC by Plato (428 BC – 348 BC, aged 80), The Academy was now 339 years old, and dominated by Epicureans and Stoics). Meanwhile, he mixed with the elite of Roman youth, such as Marcus Tullius Cicero Minor, 19, the idle son of Cicero (60), and the Pompeius (Gnaeus the Younger (75 BC – 45 BC, aged 30), Sextus (67 BC – 35 BC, aged 32)), to Sextus he later addressed a poem.

Octavius, 17, is included in Caesar's triumphal celebrations, he was put in charge of the Greek games that were staged in honor of the Temple of Venus Genetrix, built by Julius Caesar, but he was too ill to accompany his great-uncle on his Spanish campaign, against the forces of late Pompeius (106 BC – 48 BC, aged 57).

Italy, Rome, Piazza del Popolo (1822), with the Egyptian obelisk (36 m) of Sety I (1290–1279 BC) and Rameses II (1303, 1279–1213 BC) from Heliopolis, brought in 10 BC by Augustus (63 BC-14 AD) for Circus Maximus, in 1589 here.

45 BC– Vergilius, 25, begins work on the Eclogues (sometimes called the Bucolics (for its pastoral setting), about the joys of cow herding), being influenced by the greek poet Theocritus, and using Homeric hexameter.

Octavius, 18, had recovered, he sailed to the front, but was shipwrecked; after that coming ashore with a handful of companions, he crossed hostile territory to Caesar's camp (arrives in May, after the battle of Munda), which impressed his great-uncle considerably. After that time, Caesar, 55, allowed the young man to share his carriage. When back in Rome, Caesar deposited a new will with the Vestal Virgins (priestesses of Vesta, goddess of the hearth, circa 200 BC – 394, for about 600 years), naming Octavius as the prime beneficiary. Octavius is promoted to patrician rank. In October he is at Apollonia in Macedonia (in Illyria, now in Albania).

Italy, Rome, from Altare della Patria (with two pigeons): Forum Caesaris (center left, 46 BC, by Julius Caesar (100 – 44 BC), 160 m by 75 m, with Temple of Venus Genetrix (left down)), Via dei Fori Imperiali (center left), Forum Augustus (left, 2 BC).

44 BC– 15 March - Vergilius was 25 years and 5 months, when Julius Caesar (13 July 100 BC – 15 March 44 BC, aged 55.6) was assasinated by Brutus, 40.2, (Marcus Junius Brutus (June 85 BC – 23 Oct 42 BC, aged 43.2), often referred to as Brutus, was a politician of the late Roman Republic). Civil war breaks out between several parties, to get the power. Octavianus eventually emerges as the big victor, together with Marcus Antonius (14 Jan 83 BC – 1 August 30 BC, aged 53.6).

Horatius was 20.26 years old, and joined Brutus's army as a staff officer (tribunus militum (one of six senior officers of a typical legion)), because Brutus came to Athens to recruit supporters.

Octavius was 19 years old, and was appointed to replace Lepidus as magister equitum, when the Parthian expedition left. He is continuing his military studies with the legions in Illyricum, when his great-uncle, Julius Caesar, died (15 March). Octavius was named in Caesar's will as his adopted son and heir, then known as Gaius Julius Caesar Octavianus. Octavianus is announced that he is Caesar's principal heir. Caesar's soldiers at Brundisium (now Brindisi) welcome him, and he took a portion of the funds stored there. He also took an annual tribute sent to Rome from the Near Eastern province. Winning over Caesar's former veterans stationed in Campania, by June, he had gathered an army of 3,000 loyal veterans, paying each a salary of 500 denarii.

On 18 April Octavianus was at Napoli (Naples).

On 19 April: he had a meeting with Marcus Tullius Cicero, 62, (106 BC – 43 BC, aged 63.9, 27 days before 64, statesman, writer, and great orator) and Balbus, 56; then with Puteoli at Philippus' villa; and later with Cumae at Cicero's villa.

On 6 May Octavianus arrived in Rome. In early May he had a meeting with Marcus Antonius (83 BC – 30 BC, Roman politician and general), 39 years old, in Pompey's Gardens, but Antonius did not cooperate with the 19 years old Octavianus, who sponsors extravagant games in honor of Caesar, in July.

In September Cicero, 62, verbally attacked Antonius, 39, in a series of speeches.

On 28 November, Octavianus won over two of Antonius's legions (10,000 soldiers) with the enticing offer of monetary gain.

Antonius leaves for Mutina (Modena), Cisalpine Gaul, against Decimus Junius Brutus Albinus (85 BC – 43 BC, aged 42, conspirator with Marcus Brutus). Octavianus asked for support in the name of his adoptive father Caesar.

Chapter 2. Ovidius and Shakespeare

43 BC– 1 January: Octavianus, 19.2 years old, is inducted by the Senate as senator, at the urging of Cicero, 63. Octavianus also was given the power to vote alongside the former consuls. In addition, Octavianus was granted propraetor imperium (commanding power), which legalized his command of troops, sending him to relieve the siege along with Aulus Hirtius (90 BC – 21 April 43 BC, aged 47, consul and writer) and Gaius Vibius Pansa Caetronianus (12 Feb 91 BC – 43 BC, aged 48) (the consuls for 43 BC).

Octavianus' mother died, aged 42.

20 March – Publius Ovidius Naso was born in Sulmo, in an Apennine valley, 120 km east of Rome, in Roman Republic (now Sulmona, in the province of L'Aquila in Abruzzo, Italy). Ovidius's father was a respected member of the equestrian order, and schooled Ovidius very well in rhetoric, in Rome, to become an official. Ovidius had an older brother, who died at 20 years of age.

Vergilius, 26 years 5 months and 5 days, returns to Mantova, and continues to work on the Eclogues.

Horatius was 21 years, 3 months and 12 days.

14 April: battle at Forum Gallorum (25 km northwest of Bologna), Antonius was defeated.

21 April battle at Mutina, Antonius was defeated, and Hirtius and Pansa (the consuls for 43 BC) killed.

24 May: Antonius and Lepidus join forces.

19 August: First Consulate of Octavianus, 19.9, and his cousin Quintus Pedius, with the help of soldiers.

In October: meeting with Antonius and Lepidus at Island of Reni.

27 November: Second Roman Triumvirate (Antonius (40), Octavianus (20) and Lepidus (45)), legislated at Rome for 5 years. 300 senators, 2,000 equites, and other political enemies were eliminated (proscriptions).

7 December - Marcus Tullius Cicero died (3 Jan 106 BC – 7 Dec 43 BC, aged 63.9, Roman politician and orator, who served as consul in the year 63 BC). He was killed at the order of Antonius.

1564. – 23 April - After 1606 years, 1 month and 3 days, William Shakespeare was born in Stratford-upon-Avon (130 km northwest of London, and 35 km southeast of Birmingham), Warwickshire, England, to local tanner John and Mary Shakespeare. John Shakespeare was an alderman and a successful glover originally from Snitterfield, and Mary Arden was the daughter of an affluent landowning farmer. His actual birthday is unknown but assumed and celebrated today on April the 23rd, just three days before his baptism was recorded in the Parish register of the Holy Trinity Church on April the 26th.

Lope de Vega was 1 year, 6 months and 29 days old in Madrid, Spain.

42 BC– 1 January: the Senate posthumously recognized Julius Caesar as a divinity of the Roman state, Divus Julius.

Octavianus, 21, marries Clodia Pulcher (also known as Claudia, the daughter of Fulvia with her first husband Publius Clodius Pulcher. She was the stepdaughter of Marcus Antonius (who married Fulvia), and half-sister of Marcus Antonius Antyllus and Iullus Antonius, sons of Marcus Antonius with Fulvia).

Octavianus began the construction of the Temple of Divus Julius or Temple of the Comet Star, for the deification of Caesar, and added Divi Filius (Son of the Divine) to his name, becoming Gaius Julius Caesar Divi Filius.

On 23 October he and Antonius defeat Republicans under Brutus and Cassius at the Battles of Philippi (Greece), then he returns to Rome. Antonius goes to the east.

Octavianus' sister Octavia, 28, has a son, M. Claudius Marcellus.

Rome, Theatrum Marcelli (the Theatre of Marcellus (42 BC – 23 BC, nephew of the emperor Augustus), 13 BC), near the Tiber river.

Vergilius was 28 when Octavianus begins seizing farmland throughout Italy, so he can reward the men who had fought on his side in the civil war.

At the battles of Philippi, where Octavianus with Marcus Antonius win against the assassins (Brutus and his supporters) of Julius Caesar. Horatius, 22, who was staff officer for Brutus, fled from the battle, leaving behind his shield. This ended his military career, and he lost his family property. When Octavianus declared amnesty, Horatius returned to Rome, living in poverty. Soon he was appointed as a scriba quaestorius, an official at the aerarium (Treasury), and he could have some time for poetry - he began writing his Satires and Epodes (inspired from Archilochus (680 BC – 645 BC, aged 35), Greek lyric poet from the island of Paros, in the Archaic period; he is celebrated for his versatile and innovative use of poetic meters).

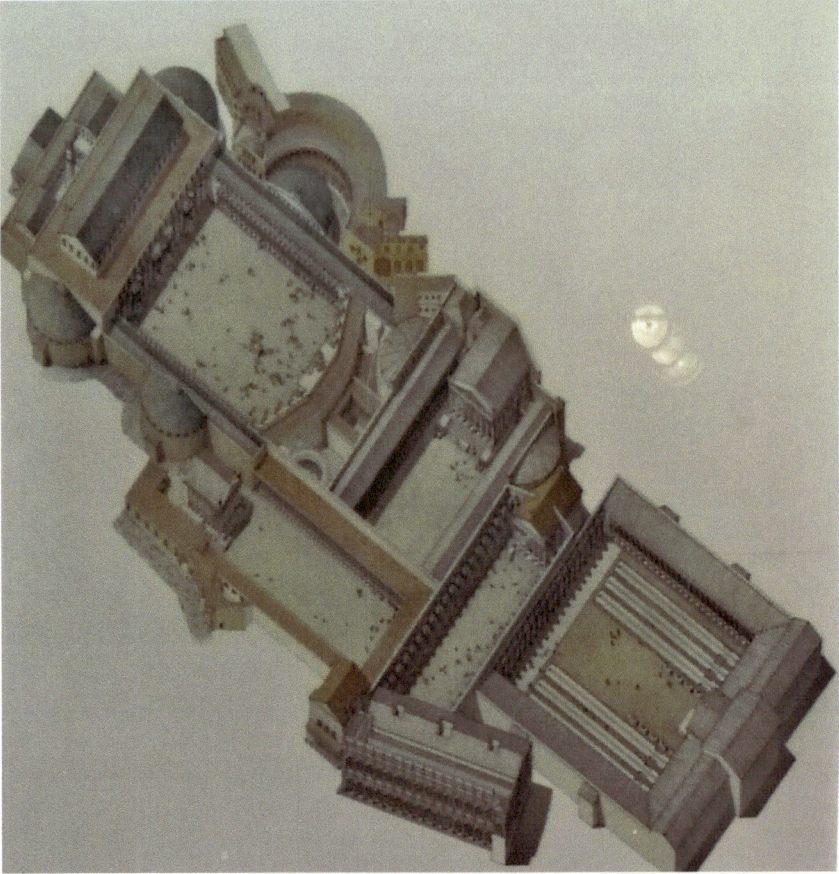

Italy, Rome (753 BC), a panel with the fife Imperial Fora (now on Via dei Fori Imperiali), which are monumental squares built in 159 years in the center of Rome: Forum Caesaris (center-left, 46 BC, with Temple of Venus Genetrix on the left, Julius Caesar (100 BC – 44 BC)), Forum Augustus (center, 2 BC, tangent and perpendicular to the southeast end of Forum Caesaris, Augustus (63 BC – 14 AD)), Forum of Vespasian (9-79) or the Temple of Peace (right down, 75 AD, 45 m southeast of Forum Augustus), Forum of Nerva (30-98) or Forum Transitorium (center-down, 98 AD, between Fora Caesaris and Augustus (northwest) and Forum of Vespasian (southeast), and Forum Traiani (up left, 113 AD, tangent to .the northeast end of Forum Caesari and to the northwest of Forum Augustus, with Columna Traiani (left up, architect Apollodorus of Damascus, 1900 years anniversary in 2013), Trajan (53 – 117, Emperor 98 – 117, attained the maximum territory).

41 BC– Vergilius, 29, lost his family's farm.

1566– 19 June - birth of King James I (19 June 1566 – 27 March 1625, aged 58.7, originally James VI of Scotland (24 July 1567 (1 year and 1 month old) – 24 March 1603, King for 35.7 years), and King of England and Ireland as James I, for 22 years, from the union of the Scottish and English crowns on 24 March 1603 until his death).

40 BC– Vergilius, 30, regained his family's farm with the help of some powerful friends and with his personal appeal to Octavianus. Then lives in Roma and Campania. He becomes friend with Horatius, 25.

Gaius Octavianus, 23, divorces Clodia Pulchra and marries Scribonia (68 BC – 16 BC, aged 52, aunt by marriage of Sextus Pompeius), now 28.

He defeats Lucius Antonius, 42, (82 BC – 39 BC, aged 43, the younger brother, and supporter, of Marcus Antonius,) at Perusia (modern Perugia). Differences between Octavianus and Antonius are resolved at Brundisium. Antonius cedes Gaul to Gaius, and is confirmed as being in charge of the eastern Roman Empire. Lepidus is sent to Africa. Antonius, 43, marries Gaius's sister, Octavia, now 28, as her second husband. They have two daughters, the younger being Antonia Minor (31 Jan 36 BC – Sep 37, aged 72.6), the mother of the 4th Roman Emperor Claudius (10 BC – 54, aged 63, emperor after Caligula (31 Aug 12 -24 Jan 41, aged 28.3, emperor 37 -41 (4 years)), 41 – 54 (13 years))

39 BC– Vergilius, 31, begins to write his first collection of ten hexameter poems, the Eclogues ("selections" in Greek), with the pastoral world that Vergilius perpetually revered, and inspiration from the Greek poet Theocritus (circa 300 BC – circa 260 BC, aged circa 40, the creator of ancient Greek bucolic poetry). Vergilius was acquainted with Maecenas, 29, (15 April 68 BC – 8 BC, aged 60), a powerful and wealthy man, advisor to Augustus, who also was the literary patron to many of Rome's most famous poets.

On 30 October, the only biological child of Gaius (Augustus), 24, the daughter Julia the Elder (known as Julia Caesaris filia or Julia Augusti filia) was born.

Treaty of Misenum between Gaius (Augustus), 24, Antonius, 44, and Sextus Pompeius, 28 (67 BC – 35 BC, aged 32) was signed.

Italy, Vatican, Basilica Papale di San Pietro (1506), an ancient Egyptian obelisk (center right, of red granite, 25.5 m, 41 m total, from Heliopolis, Egypt, 2400 BC, moved by Emperor Augustus in 30 BC to Alexandria, in 37 to Rome, here in 1586).

38 BC– Horatius, 27, was introduced, by his friend Vergilius, 32 , to Maecenas, 30, who became his close friend, and gifted him an estate near Tibur in the Sabine Hills. This estate helped Horatius to have a modest income (from five tenants), and leisure time to write.

Gaius, 25, divorces Scribonia. Scribonia will remarry, and have two more children.

Gaius replaced his praenomen "Gaius" and nomen "Julius" with Imperator, officially becoming Imperator Caesar Divi Filius.

He amasses a naval fleet to defeat Sextus Pompeius, 29, who blockaded Rome, after a victory at sea.

37 BC– Vergilius, 33, publishes Eclogues, appreciated by Maecenas, 31, literary patron also of Horatius, 28, who mentions Vergilius in his poems.

Horatius accompanied Maecenas (who wanted to negotiate the Treaty of Tarentum with Antonius) on a journey to Brundisium, described in one of his poems as a series of charming encounters with other friends along the way, such as Vergilius, but Horatius does not mention the Treaty.

Imperator Caesar Divi Filius, 26, marries Livia (58 BC – 29, aged 86) for the rest of his life (50 years). Livia Drusilla, later, after 14 AD, Julia Augusta, was 21 when she married him, she had another husband before (Tiberius Claudius Nero), for 3 years (she was 16 – 19), with whom she had two children, Tiberius, 5, (42 BC – 37, aged 78, the 2nd Roman Emperor) and Nero Claudius Drusus.

Treaty of Tarentum is signed, and the triumvirate is renewed for five years (Antonius (46), Octavianus (26) and Lepidus (51)).

Rome (753 BC): Piazza del Quirinale, with a Roman obelisk from Augustus period (27 BC – 14 AD), erected here in 1786, and Palazzo del Quirinale (center back, 1583), official residence of the President of the Italian Republic.

36 BC– Vergilius, 34, begins work on the Georgics (about the joys of farming), at the request of Maecenas, 32.

Imperator Caesar Divi Filius, 27, is granted tribunician power, strips Lepidus, 52, of all power but Pontifex Maximus (supreme priest), and expels him from triumvirate. Lepidus dies of old age (76) 24 years later, in 12 BC.

3 September: Sextus Pompeius, 31, is defeated by Agrippa, 27, (63 BC – 12 BC, aged 51, Roman consul, general, architect, close friend, son-in-low and lieutenant to Imperator (Augustus)).

35 BC– Horatius, 30, published Satires 1, which was written in hexameter verse, and described poet's rejection of public life.

Imperator Caesar Divi Filius, 28, campaigns in Illyricum.

1571. Shakespeare, 7, is likely to have begun his formal education at the local grammar school, King's New School (chartered 18 years before, in 1553), about 400 m from his home.

34 BC– Death of Gaius Sallustius Crispus, (86 BC, Amiternum, Samnium, Roman Republic (now San Vittorino, near L'Aquila, Italy)—34 BC, Rome, Roman Empire, aged 52), Roman historian, novus homo from an Italian plebeian family, and one of the great Latin literary stylists, noted for his narrative writings dealing with political personalities. Quote: "Harmony makes small things grow, lack of it makes great things decay."

Roman troops captured the Kingdom of Armenia, and Antonius, 49, made his son Alexander Helios, 6, (40 BC – circa 27 BC (aged 13), a Ptolemaic prince, the eldest son of the Macedonian queen Cleopatra VII of Ptolemaic Egypt with Roman triumvir Marcus Antonius. Alexander's fraternal twin sister was Cleopatra Selene II (40 BC – 6 BC, aged 34, had two children, buried: Royal Mausoleum of Mauretania, Sidi Rached, Algeria)) the ruler of Armenia.

1572. 11 June – birth of Ben Jonson (11 June 1572 – 6 August 1637, aged 65.1, English playwright, poet, actor, and literary critic).

33 BC: Second consulship of Imperator Caesar Divi Filius, now 30.

32 BC– Triumvirate is now at an end. Imperator Caesar Divi Filius, 31, takes upon himself the leadership of the Roman Empire, and condemns Antonius, 51, in the Senate. Antonius divorces his fourth wife Octavia, 37, the elder sister of Imperator Caesar Divi Filius, who seizes Antonius' will from the guardianship of the Vestal Virgins, and reads it in the Senate. War is declared against Cleopatra VII Philopator (69 BC – 12 August 30 BC, aged 39). Rome and the western provinces swear allegiance to Imperator Caesar Divi Filius.

Ovidius, 11, is sent by his father to study rhetoric in Rome, to become an official.

1575. - William was 11 when Queen Elizabeth, 42, (7 Sep 1533 – 24 March 1603 (aged 69.5), Queen 17 Nov 1558 – 24 March 1603 (44.3 years)) pays a visit to Kenilworth Castle (opened 1122), 20 km northeast of Stratford. There is a chance that William saw the Queen's procession, and recreated it several times later in his historical and dramatic plays.

Senate Curia (90 AD, right), Nerva's Forum (97 AD, left down, Nerva 30 - 98, Emperor 96 – 98), Basilica Aemilia (179 BC, center), Forum Romanum (295 BC, center back), Basilica Julia (for Julius Caesar, 46 BC, center back). The Forum Romanum was initially a market place, but then became the economic, political, and religious town square, and center of all Rome. The forum stood between the Palatine Hill to the east and the Capitoline Hill to the west, in the center of Rome. The Basilica Julia, which refers to Julius Caesar, probably was built by Aemilius Paullus, for Caesar, starting in 56 B.C. Its dedication was ten years later, in 46 BC, but it still wasn't finished. Augustus (63 BC – 14 AD, founder of the Roman Empire and its first Emperor from 27 BC to 14 AD) finished the building; then it burned. Augustus rebuilt it and dedicated it in 12 AD, this time to Gaius and Lucius Caesar. Probably the dedication preceded completion. A sequence of fire and rebuilding of the marble structure with wooden roof was repeated. The Basilica Julia had streets on all sides. Its dimensions: 101 meters long by 49 meters wide.

Italy, Rome (753 BC, one of the oldest continuously occupied cities in Europe, called Roma Aeterna (The Eternal City) and Caput Mundi (Capital of the World)), in Piazza Quirinale, the northeast side of Fountain of Castor (1818), with Obelisco del Quirinale (or Monte Cavallo, 1786, 29 m, from Mausoleum of Augustus (63 BC-14 AD)), and statues of the Dioscuri (Castor and Pollux, twin sons of Zeus and Leda) from the thermal baths of Constantine (272-337), Opus Phidiai on the left.

31 BC– Imperator Caesar Divi Filius, 32, had his third consulship (an office he now holds every successive year, for 8 years, until 23 BC), uses Corcyra (modern Corfu) as a Roman naval base, and defeats Marcus Antonius and Cleopatra VII at the sea battle of Actium (2 September, in Greece). Then calls himself Princeps Civitatis (First Citizen of the State).

Vergilius, 39, and Maecenas, 37, were taking turns reading the Georgics to Octavianus (Imperator Caesar Divi Filius, then Princeps Civitatis), upon his return from defeating Antonius and Cleopatra at the Battle of Actium.

1576– birth of John Weever (1576 – 1632, aged 56, English antiquary and poet, best known for his Epigrammes in the Oldest Cut, and Newest Fashion, containing epigrams on Shakespeare, Ben Jonson, and other poets of his day).

Birth of Henry Condell (1576 – Dec 1627, aged 51) actor in the King's Men, the playing company for which William Shakespeare wrote. With John Heminges (now 20 years old, also actor in the King's Men), he was instrumental in preparing and editing the First Folio, the collected plays of Shakespeare, published in 1623.

30 BC– Princeps Civitatis, 33, is in Egypt.
1 August: Princeps Civitatis defeated Antonius and Cleopatra in Alexandria.
Deaths: Antonius, 53, Cleopatra, 39, her son with Julius Caesar (in 47 BC, when she was 22, and Caesar was 53), Caesarion (now 17), and Antyllus (47 BC – 23 August 30 BC, aged 17, Antonius' eldest son).
Princeps Civitatis annexes Egypt, which becomes the private property of the emperor.

The fourth consulship of Octavianus (Princeps Civitatis) started.

Horatius, 35, published Satires 2, and the "Epodes".

29 BC– Vergilius, 41, publishes his second collection of poems, also considered one long hexameter poem, the Georgics ("On Working the Earth" in Greek) – a didactic poem, in four books, on running a farm, later supported by Augustus. It was inspired by the circa 700 years old work of the archaic Greek poet Hesiod (cica 700 BC). Vergilius dedicated this poem to Roman stateman Gaius Maecenas, 39, who had become his patron, thus Vergilius could dedicate himself to poetry. Vergilius reads from the Georgics aloud to Octavianus, 34, who also was one of Maecenas' closest friends. Vergilius' poetry quickly gained popularity for his excellent poetic skills of structure, diction and meter.

Then he started working, at the request of Octavianus, for over 10 years on Aeneid, his national epic, which remained unfinished at his death.

Princeps Civitatis, 34, builds Curia Julia., temple of Divus Julius.

28 BC: Princeps Civitatis, 35 (on 23 Sep), has the sixth consulship, with Agrippa, 35. A census takes place, and the senate is reduced.

1579– 18 December – birth of John Fletcher (18 Dec 1579 – 29 August 1625, aged 45.7, Jacobean theatre playwright, who followed William Shakespeare as house playwright for the King's Men, and was among the most prolific and influential dramatists of his day)

27 BC– Princeps Civitatis resigns his special powers, but is persuaded to continue to run the state.

On 16 January, the Roman Senate voted new titles for him, officially becoming Imperator Caesar Divi Filius Augustus, at 35 and 3 months, also becoming the first Roman emperor, and the first of the Julio-Claudian dynasty. He leaves for Gaul and Spain, and is away for two years.

Chinese silk is very popular in Rome.

Augustus creates the Praetorian Guard.

As Vergilius, 43, works on Aeneid for the rest of his life, he reads portions of it to Augustus.

Ovidius is 16 when his older brother died at 20 years of age. Then Ovidius began travelling to Athens, Asia Minor, and Sicily, and he held some minor public posts.

1580– 14 September – birth of Francisco Gómez de Quevedo y Santibáñez Villegas (14 Sep 1580 – 8 Sep 1645, aged 64.98, 6 days before 65, Spanish nobleman, politician and writer of the Baroque era. Along with Luis de Góngora (11 July 1561 – 24 May 1627, aged 65.8), Quevedo was one of the most prominent Spanish poets of the age).

A map with the Roman Empire under the Emperor Augustus (64 BC – 14 AD) on the north wall of the Basilica of Constantine, 312.

Italy, Rome (753 BC), Piazza di Monte Citorio, Camera dei Deputati (back), from Via della Guglia the view of the Obelisk of Montecitorio (or Solare, 21.79 m, 33.97 m with base and globe, moved here in 1789): an ancient Egyptian red granite obelisk of Psammetichus II (595-589 BC) from Heliopolis, brought to Rome with the Flaminian obelisk in 10 BC by the Roman Emperor Augustus (63 BC – 14 AD) to be used as the gnomon (the part of a sundial that casts the shadow) of the Solarium (or Horologium) Augusti (10 BC, functioned as a giant Solar clock, built by the mathematician Facondius Novus (circa 50 BC – 15 AD).

25 BC– Ovidius, 18, resigned from public posts, to pursue poetry, and he had his first recitation. He was part of the circle centered on the patron Marcus Valerius Messalla Corvinus, 39, (64 BC – 8 AD, aged 71, Roman general, author and patron of literature and art), and seems to have been a friend of poets in the circle of Gaius Maecenas, 43. In his writings Ovidius mentions friendships with Aemilius Macer, circa 45, (circa 70 BC in Verona – 16 BC, aged 54), Sextus Propertius, 22, (circa 47 BC – 14 BC, aged 33), and Horatius (40), and he only barely met Vergilius (45) and Albius Tibullus, 30, (circa 55 BC – 19 BC, aged 36), a fellow member of Messalla's circle, whose elegies he admired greatly. Ovidius was very popular at the time of his early poems.

M. Claudius Marcellus, now 17, marries Julia the Elder, now 16, the daughter of Augustus, 38.

Agrippa, 38, completes the Pantheon in Roma.

Italy, Rome (753 BC), on Via dei Fori Imperiali, the statue of Augustus (63 BC – 14 AD, Emperor 27 BC – 14 AD), with Forum Augustus (2 BC, back down).

1582. – 27 November - Shakespeare, 18.5, marries the older Anne Hathaway (born in 1556, 26 years old) from Shottery (1 km southwest of Stratford), at Temple Grafton, a village 8 km west from Stratford. They were together for several months before, and Anne was pregnant (3 months).

24 BC– Augustus, 39, returns to Roma, and Horatius, 41, writes very nicely about him.

1583. – 26 May – William (19) and Anne (27) Shakespeare's first child Susanna (1583 – 1649, lives 66 years) was born, just six months after Shakespeare and Anne Hathaway's wedding.

23 BC– in June, Augustus, 39.8, is ill. The conspiracy of Caepio and Murena is stopped. "Second Settlement". Augustus relinquishes the consulship, and receives full tribunician powers (tribunicia potestas) for life, and extended imperium, which is regularly renewed.

Death of Marcellus, 19, son-in-low of Augustus.

A south-west view of Rome from Altare della Patria: Theatrum Marcelli (the Theatre of Marcellus (Marcus Claudius Marcellus, 42 BC – 23 BC, Emperor Augustus' nephew), 13 BC, left back).

Vergilius, 47, recited Books 2, 4 and 6 of Aeneid to Augustus and his family.

Horatius, 42, published the first three books of his famous work, "Odes".

22 BC– Augustus, 41, refuses a dictatorship and censorship for life, but accepts a special commission. He departs for the east for three years (Athens, Ephesus, Syria, etc.).

1585. – 2 February - Shakespeare's (20.8) twins, daughter Judith (1585 – 1662, lived 77 years) and son Hamnet (1585 – 11 August 1596, lived 11.5 years), were born. Then Shakespeare probably have left his family in Stratford to join a company of actors as both playwright and performer, starting his career in theatre, and returned after 7 years, in 1592, when he was 28.

27 December – death of Pierre de Ronsard (11 Sep 1524 – 27 Dec 1585, aged 61.2, French poet, called a "prince of poets", who

revitalized the Classicism in French poetry, and was the founder of La Pléiade, an influential group of poets).

Italy, Rome (753 BC, one of the oldest cities in Europe, called Roma Aeterna (The Eternal City) and Caput Mundi (Capital of the World)), from the Pincian Hill looking southwest: Piazza del Popolo (1822), with the Egyptian obelisk (36 m) of Sety I (1290–1279 BC) and Rameses II (1303, 1279–1213 BC) from Heliopolis, brought in 10 BC by Augustus (63 BC-14 AD) for Circus Maximus, in 1589 here. Basilica San Pietro (1506, 132 m, back).

21 BC– Horatius, 44, published the first book of "Epistles", with elegant hexameter verses. In the final poem of the first book of Epistles, Horatius revealed himself to be forty-four years old in the consulship of Markus Lollius,34, (circa 55 BC – 2 AD, aged 56) and Lepidus, 39, and "of small stature, fond of the Sun, prematurely grey, quick-tempered but easily placated".

Agrippa (Marcus Vipsanius Agrippa (63 BC – 12 BC, aged 51) Roman consul, statesman, general and architect. He was the same age as Augustus, now 42, a close friend, son-in-law, and lieutenant. He helped with the construction of some of the most notable buildings in the history of Rome, and for important military victories, most notably at the Battle of Actium in 31 BC. Agrippa assisted Augustus in making Rome 'a city of marble", and renovating aqueducts to give all Romans access to the highest quality public services. He created many baths, porticoes and gardens, as well as the original Pantheon. Agrippa was also father-in-law to the second Emperor Tiberius, maternal grandfather to Caligula, and maternal great-grandfather to the 5th Roman Emperor Nero (37 – 68, aged 30.4, emperor 54 (17 years old) – 68 (13.4 years))) marries Julia the Elder (or Julia Caesaris filia or Julia Augusti filia, the daughter of Augustus, 39 BC – 14, aged 52), now 18.

20 BC– Augustus, 43, is in Asia Minor, where he makes many improvements in the administration of the provinces there.

Ovidius, 23, maybe married for the first time, but he divorced shortly.

Rome (753 BC): Piazza del Quirinale, with a Roman obelisk from Augustus period (27 BC – 14 AD), erected here in 1786 by Pius VII Pontifex Maximus (Supreme Pontiff), between two horse tamers to the left and right, and with a large water bowl in front, placed around 1850.

19 BC– Vergilius, 50.2, sets out for Greece and Asia Minor, where he planned on spending the next three years completing the Aeneid. He met the emperor Augustus in Athens, with whom he traveled to Megara, near Corinth, Greece. During his journey he became ill with fever, and returned by ship from Greece with Augustus, 43. They arrived at Brundisium.

21 September – Vergilius died of fever at Brundisium harbor, Roman Empire (now Brindisi, Italia), aged 50 years, 11 months and 6 days.

"Virgil's tomb" is found at the entrance of an ancient Roman tunnel ("grotta vecchia") in Piedigrotta, a district 3 km from the center of Naples, near the Mergellina harbor, on the road heading north along the coast to Pozzuoli.

Horatius was 45 years, 9 months and 13 days.

Ovidius was 24 years, 6 months and 1 day, and published Heroides ("Epistulae Heroidum"), 14 poems about letters of mythological heroines to their absent lovers.

Now Horatius became the most celebrated poet. Augustus, who was a prolific letter-writer, offered him the job of his private secretary, but he declined the lucrative offer, being too busy with his poems.

On 12 October, Augustus, 44, returns to Rome. The Annual Ludi Augustales is instituted to celebrate the day. Arch of Augustus is built in Rome, to commemorate victory over the Parthians.

18 BC– Agrippa, 45, receives tribunician powers.

Ovidius, 25, probably married for the second time, but divorced again.

Trajan's column (113, left), and ruins of the south-east part of Forum Traiani, and of the north-west of Augustus' Forum (13 AC).

1589. - Shakespeare, 25, probably have written his very first play, Henry VI, Part One (Henry VI (6 Dec 1421 – 21 May 1471, aged 49.6) was King of England from 1422 (9 months old) to 1461 and again from 1470 to 1471, and disputed King of France from 1422 to 1453).

17 BC– Augustus, 46, adopts his grandsons, Gaius and Lucius.

On 31 May, big celebration of Ludi Saeculares (Roman religious celebration, for three days and nights, to mark the end of a saeculum (the Roman calendar was counted Ab urbe condita ("from the foundation of the city (Rome)", AUC)), in 753 BC; and it continued in use until the Anno Domini calendar was introduced in AD 525 = 1278 Ab urbe condita, therefore 17 BC = 736 Ab urbe condita (and 2018 = 2771 Ab urbe condita), but, because of some errors and approximations in the previous 736 years, they kind of celebrated the end of the year 700 AUC, and the beginning of 701 AUC).

Despite Vergilius' deathbed supposed request that his complete (12 books in dactylic hexameter verse), yet unpolished epic Aeneid (the joy of mythological stories, with the Trojan refugee Aeneas (1200 BC, son of Goddess Aphrodite, and founder of Rome by his descendants Romulus and Remus) on Trojan ships in Carthage, Queen Dido (founder of Carthage (now in Tunisia)) asks him about the fall of Troy to the Greeks around 1150 BC, then she loves him, but Aeneas and Trojans go to Sicily, then he goes underworld, then stops at the Tiber River (on which Rome will be built), receives a shield showing all of Roman history, and finally Aeneas wins many big battles) be burned, Augustus has Vergilius' friends Varius and Tucca edit the text, and publish it two years after the death of Vergilius.

Starting from now, for over 2035 years,-generations of students learn from Vergilius' Aeneid, as it profoundly changed how the Romans, and all the cultural successors, think about poetry.

It inspired his younger contemporary, poet Ovidius, 26, whose work was reminiscent of Vergilius', but with his own aesthetic. He parodies the opening lines of the Aeneid in Amores, and his summary of the Aeneas story in Book 14 of the Metamorphoses, is called "mini-Aeneid".

Aeneid has been considered the national epic of ancient Rome from 19 BC until now. Inspired from Homer's (850 BC) Iliad and Odyssey, the Aeneid follows the Trojan refugee Aeneas as he fights to accomplish his destiny —in Roman mythology, the founding act of Rome, by his descendants Romulus and Remus. Vergilius' work has had wide influence on literature, especially the Divine Comedy (1320) of Dante Alighieri (1265 – Sep 1321, aged 56), in which Vergilius appears as Dante's guide through hell and purgatory, to the gates of Heaven.

The Aeneid was also the inspiration for John Milton's (9 Dec 1608 – 8 Nov 1674, aged 65.9) Paradise Lost (1667), which mirrored its epic structure, style and diction.

A good example of this poetic influence is this famous poem, transformed in the celebre canzonetta "Se vuoi goder la vita", composer Cesare Andrea Bixio (11 Oct 1896 – 5 March 1978, aged 81.6), sang by Beniamino Gigli (20 March 1890 – 30 Nov 1957, aged 67.6, great Italian opera tenor).

Se vuoi goder la vita

Sang by Beniamino Gigli

Una casetta in campagna,
un orticello, una vigna.
Qui chi vi nasce vi regna
non cerca e non sogna la grande cittá.
Un dolce suon di zampogna
che tanto batte nel cuore.

Se vuoi goder la vita
vieni quaggiú in campagna,
é tutta un'altra cosa
vedi il mondo color di rosa,
quest'aria deliziosa
non é l'aria della cittá.

Svegliati con il gallo,
specchiati nel ruscello,
bacia la tua compagna
che t'accompagna col somarello.
Ogni figliolo è un fiore nato sulla colina,
baciane una dozzina. Oh! Che felicitá.

Se vuoi goder la vita
torna al tuo paesello
ch'é assai piú bello della cittá.

Fasci lucenti di grano
sembra ogni falce un baleno,
tutto un sapore nostrano,
profumo di fieno di grappoli e fior.
E la sorgente pian piano
mormora un canto d'amore.

Se vuoi goder la vita
vieni quaggiú in campagna,
é tutta un'altra cosa
vedi il mondo color di rosa,
quest'aria deliziosa
non é l'aria della cittá.

Svegliati con il gallo,
specchiati nel ruscello,
bacia la tua compagna
che t'accompagna col somarello,
ogni figliolo è un fiore, nato sulla colina,
baciane una dozzina. Oh! Che felicitá.

Se vuoi goder la vita
torna al tuo paesello
ch'é assai piú bello della cittá!

Vergilius's quotes: The greatest wealth is health.
Fortune sides with him who dares.

Emperor Augustus, 46, asked Horatius, 48, to write a ceremonial poem celebrating his reign, to be sung in the temple of Apollo for the Secular Games, an old festival that Augustus revived, in his desire of recreating ancient customs – the poem is Carmen Saeculare, a hymn in Sapphic meter, and was published in 17 BC.

Ovidius, 26, began publishing his first major work "Amores" as a five-book collection.

Trajan's Market (113 AD, left), Augustus' Forum (12 AD, center), and policemen on horses.

1590. – Shakespeare, 26, probably have written Henry VI, Part Two, and Henry VI, Part III.

16 BC– Ovidius, 27, published the first five-book collection of the Amores, a series of erotic poems addressed to a lover, Corinna.

Augustus, 47, departs for Gaul and Spain for three years, with his wife Livia, 42, her son Tiberius, 26, and Terentia, the wife of Maecenas.

1591. – 23 August – death of Fray Luis de León (1527 – 23 August 1591, aged 64, Spanish lyric poet, Augustinian friar, theologian and academic, active during the Spanish Golden Age).

1592. - Shakespeare, 28, probably returned to his family in Stratford. Then probably he goes to London, where he begins to be noticed as a personality within London theatre; Robert Greene's *Groatworth of Wit* called Shakespeare an "upstart crow". He attacks Shakespeare as lacking originality, since he borrows ideas from others for his own plays.

Theatres in London close because of the plague.

Shakespeare probably have written the poem *Venus and Adonis* and the plays *Richard III* (2 Oct 1452 – 22 Aug 1485 (aged 32.9) King of England (for 2.1 years) from 1483 (age 30.7) until his death in the Battle of Bosworth Fieldand), *The Two Gentlemen of Verona.*

Also *The Comedy of Errors* maybe was written in this time.

13 September – death of Michel de Montaigne (28 Feb 1533 – 13 Sep 1592, aged 59.6, French philosopher and essayist).

14 BC– Lucius Orbilius Pupillus died (114 BC – 14 BC, aged 100) was a Latin grammarian of the 1st century BC, who taught at school, first at Benevento and then at Rome, where Horatius, around 10 years old, in 55 BC, was his pupil, Orbilius being then around 59). Horatius was 51.

1593. - Shakespeare, 29, began to compose the first of what will amount to a 154 sonnet collection. His narrative poem *Venus and Adonis* is his first ever published. *The Rape of Lucrece, Titus Andronicus* and *The Taming of the Shrew* probably were also started by Shakespeare at this time.

13 BC– Ovidius, 30, married for the third time, and had one daughter, who eventually bore him grandchildren. This third and last wife was connected in some way to the influential gens Fabia, and would help him during his exile in Tomis, after 8 AD.

Augustus, 50, returns to Rome.

Lepidus dies. Marcus Aemilius Lepidus (89 BC – 13 BC, aged 76), was a Roman patrician, who was in a triumvirate with Octavianus (Augustus) and Marcus Antonius, and the last Pontifex Maximus of the Roman Republic. Lepidus had previously been a close ally of Julius Caesar.

Italy, Rome (753 BC), from Via del Teatro di Marcello, Theatrum Marcelli (Marcus Claudius Marcellus, 42 BC – 23 BC, 19 years, nephew of the emperor Augustus, who named this theatre after him in 13 BC)), 250 m northeast of the Tiber river.

1594. - Shakespeare, 30, The Lord Chamberlain's Men, a theatre troupe, including distinguished actor Richard Burbage and comic Will Kemp, performed with Shakespeare in their group.

Shakespeare probably started *Love Labour's Lost,* and *King John* (24 Dec 1166 – Oct 1216 (aged 49.9), King of England 6 April 1199 – Oct 1216 (17 years)).

12 BC– Horatius, 53, began to write the critical, "Ars Poetica". In a verse epistle to Augustus (Epistle 2.1), Horatius argued for classic status to be awarded to contemporary poets, including Vergilius and maybe himself.

Augustus, 51, was elected Pontifex Maximus of the Roman Empire, because Lipidus died at 76.

Agrippa died at 51.

Italy, Cividale del Friuli, 3 Nov 2009, Palazzo Comunale (1350-1550), left Campanile con orologio, right Giulio Caesare (100 BC – 44 BC) statue.

1595. - Shakespeare, 31, probably wrote *Richard II* (6 Jan 1367 in Bordeaux, France – 14 Feb 1400 (aged 33.1), also known as Richard of Bordeaux, was King of England for 22.1 years, from 1377 (when he was 10.5 years old) until he was deposed on 30 September 1399), performed that very same year, *A Midsummer Night's Dream*, probably composed for a wedding, and the greatest love story *Romeo and Juliet.*

25 April – death of Torquato Tasso (11 March 1544, Sorento, Kingdom of Napoli (Naples), Italy – 25 April 1595, Rome, Italy, aged 51.1, greatest Italian poet of the late Renaissance, renowned for his heroic epic poem Gerusalemme liberata (1581; "Jerusalem Liberated")).

11 BC– Horatius, 54, published the second book of "Epistles", and the fourth book of "Odes".

Tiberius (Tiberius Claudius Nero, 42 BC – 37, son of the current wife of Augustus, with her previous husband), now 31, divorces his wife, Agrippa's daughter with Pomponia Caecilia Attica, and marries Julia the Elder, 28, the daughter of Augustus, becoming son-in-low of Augustus.

Death of Octavia (circa 68 BC – 11 BC, aged 57), the sister of Augustus.

On 4 May: grand opening of the Theater of Marcellus.

Italy, Roma, Theatrum Marcelli (the Theatre of Marcellus (Marcus Claudius Marcellus, 42 BC – 23 BC, aged 19, nephew of the emperor Augustus, who named this theatre after him in 11 BC)), near the Tiber river.

1596. Shakespeare, 32, probably wrote *The Merry Wives of Windsor*. The theatre troupe The Lord Chamberlain's Men lost their original patron, Henry Carey, also Lord Hunsdon and Lord Chamberlain, and they were replaced by the brother George Carey, and Second Lord Hunsdon, who succeeds his late brother.

Shakespeare probably started *The Merchant of Venice,* and *Henry IV, Part One* (15 April 1367 – 20 March 1413 (aged 45.9), also known as Henry of Bolingbroke, was King of England and Lord of Ireland for 13.5 years, from 1399 to 1413).

10 BC– Ovidius, 33, probably had the premiere of his tragedy Medea, which was admired in antiquity, but is no longer surviving.

Herod (73 BC – 4 BC, aged 69, Roman-appointed king in Middle East (37 BC (at 36) – 4 BC, for 33 years), who built many fortresses, aqueducts, theatres, and other public buildings) names his new city Caesarea (now on Israel's Mediterranean coast) in honor of Augustus.

Statue of Augustus as Pontifex Maximus is sculpted.

Trajan's Market (113 AC, back) and ruins of the south-east part of Forum Traiani, and of the north-west part of Augustus' Forum (13 AC).

1597. - Shakespeare, 33, bought the New Place, one of Stratford's most preeminent homes. This generated speculation for long time, by many academics and other people, that William Shakespeare was really a successful businessman, and not literature's celebrated playwright.

1598. - Shakespeare, 34, probably wrote the play *Henry IV, Part Two,* and his reputation as an actor is confirmed by his performance in Ben Jonson's *Every Man in his Humor,* which clearly lists his name as a principal actor in the London play.

William wrote the play *Much Ado About Nothing* in this year.

9 BC: A massive altar, the Ara Pacis, is completed and dedicated by Augustus, 54, in Rome.

Death of Drusus, Tiberius's younger brother.

France, Lyon (43 BC, by Munatius Plancus (87 BC – 15 BC) and Lepidus (77 BC – 11 BC), lieutenants of Julius Caesar (100 BC – 44 BC)), part of eastern façade of the Hôtel de Ville (1645 – 1651, 1674) de Lyon, in Place de la Comédie, across Opéra.

8 BC– Horatius, 56.2, published "Ars Poetica".
In the summer Maecenas, 60, died.
27 November – Quintus Horatius Flaccus died in Rome, Roman Empire, aged 56 years 11 months and 19 days (11 days before 57).

He was buried near the tomb of Maecenas.

Horatius had no heirs, and, as Maecenas, he left his estate to Augustus.

Ovidius was 35 years, 8 months and 7 days.

The most frequent themes in Horatius' works were love, pleasures of friendship and simple life, and the art of poetry. His most important work is "Ars Poetica", which influenced many playwrights and writers including:

- Lope de Vega (25 Nov 1562 – 27 August 1635, aged 72.7, Spanish playwright, poet and novelist),

- Michel de Montaigne (28 Feb 1533 – 13 Sep 1592, aged 59.6, French philosopher and essayist),

- Henry Fielding (22 April 1707 – 8 Oct 1754, aged 47.5, English novelist and dramatist, known for his earthy humor and satirical ability, and as the author of the novel Tom Jones (1749)),

- Pedro Calderón de la Barca (17 Jan 1600 – 25 May 1681, aged 81.3, Spanish dramatist, poet and writer),

- Pierre Corneille (6 June 1606 – 1 Oct 1684, aged 78.3, French tragedian, generally considered one of the three great seventeenth-century French dramatists, along with Molière (15 Jan 1622 – 17 Feb 1673, aged 51.1, full name Jean-Baptiste Poquelin, known by his stage name Molière, a French playwright, actor and poet, regarded as one of the greatest writers in the French language and universal literature) and Jean Racine (22 Dec 1639 – 21 April 1699, aged 59.3, French dramatist),

- Samuel Johnson (18 Sep 1709 – 13 Dec 1784, aged 75.2, often referred to as Dr. Johnson, an English poet, essayist, moralist, literary critic, biographer, editor and lexicographer),

- Johann Wolfgang von Goethe (28 August 1749 – 22 March 1832, aged 82.6, German poet, playwright, novelist, scientist, statesman, theatre director, critic, and amateur artist. His works include epic and lyric poetry; prose and verse dramas; memoirs; an autobiography; literary and aesthetic criticism; treatises on botany, anatomy, and color; and four novels. Quote: Knowing is not enough; we must apply. Willing is not enough; we must do.),

- Voltaire (21 Nov 1694 – 30 May 1778, aged 83.5, full name François-Marie Arouet, known by his nom de plume Voltaire, a French writer, historian and philosopher, famous for his wit, and his attacks on the establishment. He insisted on the freedom of religion, freedom of speech, and separation of church and state. Quote: Those who can make you believe absurdities, can make you commit atrocities.),

- Denis Diderot (5 Oct 1713 – 31 July 1784, aged 70.7, French philosopher, art critic, and writer, best known for serving as co-founder, chief editor, and contributor to the Encyclopédie, along with Jean le Rond d'Alembert.(16 Nov 1717 – 29 Oct 1783, aged 65.9, French mathematician, mechanician, physicist, philosopher, and music theorist. Until 1759 he was also co-editor with Denis Diderot of the Encyclopédie).

Horatius' works also deeply influenced later writers including

- Ben Jonson (11 June 1572 – 6 August 1637, aged 65.1, English playwright, poet, actor, and literary critic),

- Alexander Pope (21 May 1688 – 30 May 1744, aged 56 years and 9 days, height only 1 m and 37 cm, English poet with satirical verse, and translator of Homer (circa 850 BC, Greek author of The Iliad and The Odyssey)),

- Mihai Eminescu (15 Jan 1850 – 15 June 1889, aged 39 and 5 months, Romantic poet, novelist and journalist, generally regarded as the most famous and influential Romanian poet),

- Robert Frost (26 March 1874, San Francisco, CA – 29 Jan 1963, Boston, MA, aged 88.8, an American poet, initially published in England, before it was published in America. Known for his realistic depictions of rural life, and his command of American colloquial speech, Frost frequently wrote about settings from rural life in New England, around Boston).

- W.H. Auden (21 Feb 1907 in York, UK – 29 Sep 1973 in Vienna, Austria, aged 66.6, English-American poet distinguished for its stylistic and technical achievement).

Horatius' other important works were "Odes", "Epodes", "Satires", "Epistles", and "Carmen Saeculare".

Horatius' poetry themes like the beatus ille (an appraisal of simple life), and carpe diem ("enjoy the day") gained importance to this day, and influenced poets like

- Ovidius (21 years younger, who followed his example in creating a completely natural style of expression in hexameter verse),

- Francesco Petrarca (20 July 1304, Arezzo, Toscana, Italy – 19 July 1374, Arquà Petrarca, near Padua, Carrara Italy, aged 69.99, one day before 70, anglicized as Petrarch, was an Italian scholar, poet and humanist in Renaissance Italy. His rediscovery of Cicero's letters is credited with initiating the 14th-century Renaissance. He is considered the founder of Humanism. Quotes: "To be able to say how much you love is to love but little". "Five great enemies of peace inhabit with us — avarice, ambition, envy, anger and pride; if these were to be banished, we should infallibly enjoy perpetual peace".

- Dante Alighieri (30 May 1265, Firenze, Italy – 14 Sep 1321, Ravenna, Italy, aged 56.3), Italian poet, prose writer, literary theorist, moral philosopher, and political thinker, best known for the monumental epic poem La commedia, later named La divina commedia (The Divine Comedy, 1320), in which Vergilius appears as Dante's guide through hell and purgatory, to the gates of Heaven. The great Renaissance poet, was pardoned in 2008 by Firenze (Florence) – from where he was exiled on pain of death in 1302 (at age 37), 706 years ago.

- Garcilaso de la Vega (1501, Toledo, Spain – 14 Oct 1536, Nice, France, aged 35, Spanish soldier and the most influential poet to introduce Italian Renaissance verse forms, poetic techniques, and themes to Spain),

- Juan Boscán i Almogàver (1490, Barcelona, Spain – 21 Sep 1542, Barcelona, Spain, aged 52, Spanish poet who incorporated hendecasyllable verses into Spanish,

- Torquato Tasso (11 March 1544, Sorento, Kingdom of Napoli (Naples), Italy – 25 April 1595, Rome, Italy, aged 51.1, greatest Italian poet of the late Renaissance, renowned for his heroic epic poem Gerusalemme liberata (1581; "Jerusalem Liberated"), describing the capture of Jerusalem during the First Crusade (1096 – 1099), called for by French Pope Urban II (c 1035 – 29 July 1099, aged circa 64, Pope for 11.3 years, from 12 March 1088 to his death) at the Council of Clermont in 1095).

- Pierre de Ronsard (11 Sep 1524 – 27 Dec 1585, aged 61.2, French poet, called a "prince of poets", who revitalized the Classicism in French poetry, and was the founder of La Pléiade, an influential group of poets),

- Fray Luis de León (1527 – 23 August 1591, aged 64, Spanish lyric poet, Augustinian friar, theologian and academic, active during the Spanish Golden Age),
- Shakespeare,
- Francisco Gómez de Quevedo y Santibáñez Villegas (14 Sep 1580 – 8 Sep 1645, aged 64.98, 6 days before 65, Spanish nobleman, politician and writer of the Baroque era. Along with Luis de Góngora (11 July 1561 – 24 May 1627, aged 65.8), Quevedo was one of the most prominent Spanish poets of the age).

Horace's Ars Poetica is second only to Aristotle's Poetics in its influence on literary theory and criticism.

Horace is also well known for creating several Latin phrases that are still in use today, whether in Latin or translation. These phrases include carpe diem, Dulce et decorum est pro patria mori (It is sweet and fitting to die for one's country), Nunc est bibendum (Now we must drink), and aurea mediocritas ("golden mediocrity").

Italy, Gate 2 to the ruins of Pompeii (650 BC, in 79 covered by ash), with a panel entitled CARPE DIEM (enjoy the day), a Latin aphorism from a poem in the Odes (book 1, number 11) in 23 BC by the Roman poet Horace (Quintus Horatius Flaccus, born December 8, 65 BC in Venusia, Roman Republic, died November 27, 8 BC, in Rome, the capital of the Roman Empire). Important lyric poetry volumes are Odes, Satires and Ars Poetica.

1599. – Shakespeare is 35 when the Major shareholders of the theater troupe The Lord Chamberlain's Men lease land from Nicholas Brend, and The Globe Theatre opened later that same year.

25 April - Oliver Cromwell was born. He was an English military and political leader, and served for 5 years as Lord Protector of the Commonwealth of England, Scotland, and Ireland, from 1653 until his death on 3 Sep 1658, aged 59.3.

21 September - *Julius Caesar* was performed at the Globe Theatre for the first known time, according to German tourist Thomas Platter's diary.

John Weever, 23, (1576 – 1632, aged 56, English antiquary and poet, best known for his Epigrammes in the Oldest Cut, and Newest Fashion, containing epigrams on Shakespeare, Ben Jonson, and other poets of his day) praises Shakespeare's *Romeo and Juliet, The Rape of Lucrece* and *Venus Adonis* in the poem *Ad Guglielmum Shakespeare.*

Map of Foro di Nerva (30 – 98 AD, Roman Emperor 96 – 98). The Forum was inaugurated in 97 AD and was located between the Forum of Augustus (63 BC – 14 AD, first Roman Emperor 27 BC – 14 AD) to north-west, the Forum of Caesar (100 BC – 44 BC, 46 BC) to west, Forum of Vespasian (9 AD – 79, Roman Emperor 69 - 79) with Temple Pacis (Temple of Peace) to south-east, Basilica Emilia (179 BC) to south and Forum Romanum to south-west.

In this photo only the south part of some of the ruins of the Forum of Nerva are visible, with the Forum of Augustus out of the photo to the left, the Forum of Caesar behind and to the right of the photo, a small wall of the Temple Pacis is on the center-left, below the Amphitheatrum Flavium (Colosseum, 80 AD), Basilica Emilia and Forum Romanum are to the right. The walls on the left and in the center are from aristocratic houses of the Charlemagne period (800 – 888). Basilica of Maxentius (312) and the churches Santi Cosma e Damiano and San Lorenzo are in the back.

1600. - Shakespeare, 36, probably wrote his greatest play, *Hamlet*.

17 January – birth of Pedro Calderón de la Barca (17 Jan 1600 – 25 May 1681, aged 81.3, Spanish dramatist, poet and writer).

1601. - Shakespeare, 37, probably wrote the narrative poem, *The Phoenix and the Turtle*, and *Twelfth Night or What You Will*.

5 BC– Ovidius, 38, published the surviving second version of Amores, redacted to three books, instead of the original five books.

Twelfth consulship of Augustus, 58.

1602. - Shakespeare, 38, probably wrote All Well That Ends Well, and Troilus and Cressida.

2 May – birth of Athanasius Kircher (2 May 1602 – 28 November 1680, aged 78.5), German Jesuit scholar and polymath, who published around 40 major works, most notably in the fields of comparative religion, geology, and medicine). He also made a map of Atlantis, in 1669 (age 67), placing it in the middle of the Atlantic Ocean, published in Mundus Subterraneus, in Amsterdam. The map is oriented with south at the top, and north down. Atlantis, a probable mythical island nation mentioned in Plato's (427 BC – 347 BC, aged 80) dialogues "Timaeus" and "Critias," (360 BC) has been an object of interest among western philosophers and historians for over 2,300 years. Plato describes it as a powerful and advanced kingdom that sank, in a night and a day, into the ocean around 9600 BC. The ancient Greeks were divided as to whether Plato's story was to be considered as history or mere symbol. Since the 19th century there has been renewed interest in linking Plato's Atlantis to historical locations, most commonly the Greek South Aegean island of Santorini (130 km north of the Crete Island, and 220 km southeast of Athens), which was destroyed by a volcanic eruption around 1600 BC. Plato (through the character Critias in his dialogues) describes Atlantis as an island larger than Libya and Asia Minor put together, located in the Atlantic just beyond the Pillars of Hercules— generally assumed to mean the Strait of Gibraltar. Its culture was advanced, and it had a constitution questionably similar to the one

outlined in Plato's "Republic." It was protected by the god Poseidon, who made his son Atlas king, and namesake of the island, and the ocean that surrounded it. As the Atlanteans grew powerful, their ethics declined. Their armies eventually conquered Africa as far as Egypt and Europe as far as Tyrrhenia (Etruscan Italy), before being driven back by an Athenian-led alliance. Later, by way of divine punishment, the island was beset by earthquakes and floods, and sank into a muddy sea. Plato's Critias says he heard the story of Atlantis from his grandfather, who had heard it from the Athenian statesman and poet Solon (640 BC – 558 BC, aged 82, 150 years before Plato's time), who had learned it from an Egyptian priest, who said it had happened 9000 years before that. Plato's intent in telling this story seems to have been to boost his ideas of an ideal society, using stories of ancient victory and calamity, to call to mind more recent events such as Athens' disastrous invasion of Sicily in 415 BC - 413 BC. The historicity of Plato's tale was controversial in ancient times — his follower Crantor (350 BC – 276 BC, aged 74) is said to have believed it, while Strabo (63 BC – 23 AD, aged 85, Greek geographer) records Aristotle's (384 BC – 322 BC, aged 62) joke about Plato's ability to conjure nations out of thin air, and then destroy them. From time to time, archaeologists and historians locate evidence—a swampy, prehistoric city in coastal Spain; a suspicious undersea rock formation in the Bahamas — that might be a source of the Atlantis story. Of these, the site with the widest acceptance is the Greek island of Santorini (ancient Thera), a half-submerged caldera created by the massive second-millennium-B.C. volcanic eruption, whose tsunami may have hastened the collapse of the Minoan civilization on Crete.

4 BC. – Lucius Annaeus Seneca was born (4 BC - 65 AD, aged 68), Roman Stoic philosopher, statesman and dramatist.

1603. – Shakespeare was 39 when *A Midsummer's Night* was performed at Hampton Court (Hampton Court Palace is a royal palace in the borough of Richmond upon Thames, London, England, 18.8 km) southwest and upstream of central London on the River Thames. Building of the palace began in 1515 for Cardinal Thomas Wolsey, a favorite of King Henry VIII (28 June 1491 – 28 Jan 1547, aged 55.5, King of England for 37.7 years, from 21 April 1509 (17.8

years old) until his death) before Queen Elizabeth, 69.4, who dies later that year.

24 March – death of Queen Elizabeth, 69.5, (7 Sep 1533 – 24 March 1603 (aged 69.5), Queen 17 Nov 1558 – 24 March 1603 (44.3 years))

24 March – the new King is James I (19 June 1566 – 27 March 1625, aged 58.7, originally James VI of Scotland (24 July 1567 (1 year and 1 month old) – 24 March 1603, King for 35.7 years), and King of England and Ireland as James I, for 22 years, from the union of the Scottish and English crowns on 24 March 1603 until his death). He proved to be an enthusiastic patron of the arts, granting the theater troupe *The Chamberlain's Men* a patent to perform. In return the Company renames itself *The King's Men* to honor James I, and they quickly become a favorite with the new king.

As You Like It was performed by the newly named King's Men before King James I at Wilton (5 km west of Salisbury, 130 km southwest of London).

Shakespeare was recorded as performing in Ben Jonson's (31 years old, (11 June 1572 – 6 August 1637, aged 65.1, English playwright, poet, actor, and literary critic)) *Sejanus*, which is Shakespeare's last recorded acting performance.

3 BC– Ovidius, 40, probably published the Medicamina Faciei, a fragmentary work on women's beauty treatments.

1604. - Shakespeare, 40, probably wrote *Measure for Measure*. It was later performed at King James I Court.

He also probably wrote Othello, which was performed on

1 November - Othello was performed at Whitehall (in Westminster, London, 600 m north of Westminster Abbey).

2 BC: Thirteenth consulship of Augustus, 61. He inaugurates the Forum Augustum and the Temple of Mars Ultor in Rome, to commemorate his victory at the Battle of Philippi in 42 BC. Augustus is declared Pater Patriae ("Father of His Country").

His daughter Julia the Elder, 37, married with Tiberius for 9 years, is banished for adultery to Pandateria (now Ventotene, one of the Pontine Islands in the Tyrrhenian Sea, 50 km west of Napoli

(Naples)), from which she is allowed, after over 5 years, in AD 4 to move to Rhegium Julium (now Reggio Calabria, a coastal city in southern Italy, separated from Messina in Sicily by the Strait of Messina).

Forum Nervae (97, down), Forum Augusti (2 BC, with Temple of Mars Ultor, built with white marble of Carrara, center-right-up).

1605. – Shakespeare was 41 when *The Merchant of Venice* was performed twice at King James' Court, earning a commendation from the King.

Shakespeare probably wrote King Lear, and Macbeth (1005 – 15 August 1057, aged 52, King of Scots for 17 years, from 1040 until his death. He was titled King of Alba during his life, and ruled only over a portion of present-day Scotland), the play's Scottish background, and kind portrayal of ancestor Malcolm being intended as a celebration, and honoring of King James Scottish ancestry.

1 BC– Ovidius, 42, publishes the first volume of "Ars Amatoria", the Art of Love, a parody of didactic poetry, and a three-book manual about seduction and intrigue.

1606. - Shakespeare, 42, probably wrote Antony and Cleopatra.

6 June – birth of Pierre Corneille (6 June 1606 – 1 Oct 1684, aged 78.3, French tragedian).

26 December – first performance of King Lear.

1 AD– Ovidius, 43, publishes the second and third volumes of "Ars Amatoria".

Augustus's first grandson Gaius Caesar (20 BC – 4 in Lycia, now Turkey, aged 23), now 20, is on a mission to Syria, and is a consul.

UK, London: Inside (southwest) the British Museum, The Lion of Knidos (350 BC, 7 t, found May 1858 in the ancient cemetery of Knidos, a coastal city in south-west Turkey, marble from Mt Pendelikon near Athens).

1607. – Shakespeare was 43 when *Hamlet* and *Richard III* were performed aboard the British ship *Dragon* off the west coast of Africa, at Sierra Leone.

Shakespeare probably started *Timon of Athens* (circa 450 BC – circa 380 BC) had a reputation for reclusiveness, which grew to legendary status. According to the historian Plutarch (46 – 120, aged 74), Timon lived during the era of the Peloponnesian War (431 BC – 404 BC), and was the wealthy son of Echecratides, who lavished his money on flattering friends. When his funds ran out, the friends deserted him, and Timon was reduced to working in the fields. One day, he found a pot of gold, and soon his fair-weather friends were back. This time, he drove them away with dirt clods.),

Pericles (494 BC – 429 BC, aged 65, a prominent and influential Greek statesman, orator, general and patron of the arts of Athens during the Golden Age — specifically 31 years (460 BC – 429 BC) the time between the Persian (499 BC – 449 BC) and Peloponnesian wars (431 BC – 404 BC). Quotes: What you leave behind is not what is engraved in stone monuments, but what is woven into the lives of others. Just because you do not take an interest in politics doesn't mean politics won't take an interest in you. Freedom is the sure possession of those alone who have the courage to defend it.), and

Coriolanus (Gaius Marcius Coriolanus (circa 520 BC – circa 450 BC) - Roman general who led the Roman troops in a siege of the Volscian city of Corioli (central Italy, south of Rome) in 493 BC. Later, not being appreciated by his countrymen, he deserted to the enemy).

Shakespeare's daugther Susanna, 24, (1583 – 1649, aged 66 years) married a physician, John Hall.

2 AD– Ovidius, 44, published the "Remedia Amoris".

Augustus's second grandson Lucius Caesar, born in 17 BC, dies in Marseille (now France), aged 18. Place of burial is Mausoleum of Augustus in Rome. It was intended that he and his older brother Gaius Caesar should rule the Roman Empire together, after the death of their grandfather Augustus.

Tiberius, 44, son, from a previous marriage, of the wife of Augustus, returns to Rome from Rhodes, island in Greece, 50 km southwest of Turkey, 1,500 km southeast of Rome.

Italy, Rome (753 BC, one of the oldest continuously occupied cities in Europe, called Roma Aeterna (The Eternal City) and Caput Mundi (Capital of the World)), in Piazza Quirinale, the northeast side of Fountain of Castor (1818), with Obelisco del Quirinale (or Monte Cavallo, 1786, 29 m, from Mausoleum of Augustus (63 BC-14 AD)), and statues of the Dioscuri (Castor and Pollux, twin sons of Zeus and Leda) from the thermal baths of Constantine (272-337), Opus Phidiai on the left.

1608. – Shakespeare was 44 when the theater troupe The King's Men takes on a twenty-one year lease of London's first permanently enclosed theatre, the Blackfriars Theatre (1597, Blackfriars Theatre was the name given to two separate theatres located in the former Blackfriars Dominican monastery (1275) in the City of London). Notes on stage directions, suggest *The Tempest* was written by Shakespeare with a performance at this theatre in mind.

The return of the plague forces a closure for two years of all playhouses and theatres, from the spring of 1608 through to early 1610.

9 December – John Milton was born in Cheapside, City of London, UK. He was an English poet, polemicist, man of letters, and civil servant for the Commonwealth of England under Oliver Cromwell (25 April 1599 – 3 Sep 1658, aged 59.3). Died on 8 Nov 1674, aged 65.9.

1609. - Shakespeare, 45, probably started Cymbeline (about Cunobelinus (circa 20 BC – 42 AD, king in pre-Roman Britain from about AD 10 until about AD 42. He was a ruler of a large area of southeastern Britain. The play's imaginary plot bears no relation to the events in Cunobelinus' career.).

4: Augustus's first grandson Gaius Caesar, born in 20 BC, dies in Lycia, now Turkey, aged 24.

Tiberius, 46, is adopted by Augustus, 66.

Tiberius adopts his nephew Germanicus (15 BC – 19, aged 34, son of Tiberius's brother Nero Claudius Drusus and Antonia Minor), now 19. Tiberius receives tribunician powers for ten years.

Italy, Rome (753 BC), Forum Romanum, the south half of the northwest side of Arcus Septimii Severi (left, 203, Septimius Severus (145 – 211)), the northeast side of Temple Saturni (center right, 497 BC, 42 BC, 380), Basilica Juliae (center back, 54 BC by Julius Caesar (100 – 44 BC), fluted Corinthian Column of Phocas (center left, 350 BC, 13 m, rededicated 1 August 608 to the Eastern (Byzantine) Roman Emperor Flavius Phocas (born 547, Emperor 602-610), the last Imperial monument in this Forum).

1610. – Shakespeare was 46 when Othello was performed at Oxford College, by the King's Men, during a summer tour.
Shakespeare probably started The Winter's Tale.

1611. - Shakespeare, 47, probably wrote The Tempest.

6: Augustus, 68, creates the aerarium militare, a treasury drawn from taxes, in order to fund a professional army. He also creates Rome's permanent firefighting force, the Vigiles, under a Praefectus.
Judaea is made a province of Rome. Provinces of Sardinia (with Corsica) and Moesia (Roman province situated in the Balkans, along the south bank of the Danube River. It included most of the

territory of modern-day Central Serbia, and the northern parts of the modern Republic of Macedonia (Moesia Superior), as well as Northern Bulgaria and Romanian Dobrudja (the southeast part of Romania, between the Danube River to the west and north, and the Black Sea to the east) (Moesia Inferior)) are transferred to the emperor.

1612. – Shakespeare was 48 when The King's Men performed Othello and Julius Caesar, amongst others.

Shakespeare probably wrote Cardenio (based on the first volume from Miguel de Cervantes's (29 Sep 1547 – 22 April 1616, aged 68.4, the greatest writer in the Spanish language, and one of the world's best novelists) masterpiece Don Quixote (first volume published in 1605, in English in 1612, second volume in 1615, in English in 1620)), his only lost play, during this period, and, with John Fletcher, 33, (18 Dec 1579 – 29 August 1625, aged 45.7, Jacobean theatre playwright, who followed William Shakespeare as house playwright for the King's Men, and was among the most prolific and influential dramatists of his day) as a likely contributor, composed Henry VIII (28 June 1491 – 28 Jan 1547, aged 55.5, King of England for 37.7 years, from 21 April 1509 (17.8 years old) until his death)).

1613. – Shakespeare was 49 when Cardenio was performed by the King's Men, and The Globe Theatre burned to the ground.

He probably retired to Stratford, and partially wrote The Two Noble Kinsmen. 21 years later, a 1634 entry within the Stationer's Registry confirmed that both William Shakespeare and John Fletcher composed this play.

London, UK: On Sermon Lane, 100 m south of St. Paul's Cathedral, The National Firefighters Memorial (1991, by John W. Mills (born 1933)).

8 – Ovidius, 50 had completed his masterpiece, "Metamorphoses", an epic poem in fifteen books derived from Greek mythology about mythical figures who have undergone transformations (from the emergence of the cosmos from formless mass to the organized, material world, to famous myths such as Apollo and Daphne, Daedalus and Icarus, Orpheus and Eurydice, and Pygmalion, to the deification of Julius Caesar). It is written in dactylic hexameter, the epic meter of Homer's "Odyssey" and "Iliad" and Vergilius' "Aeneid". It remains an invaluable source on Roman religion, and explains many myths alluded to in other works.

At the same time, Ovidius worked on the Fasti, a six-book poem in elegiac couplets on the theme of the calendar of Roman festivals and astronomy. The composition of this poem was interrupted by Ovidius' exile, and it is thought that Ovidius abandoned work on the piece in Tomis.

Ovidius, 50, was exiled by Augustus to Tomis, Scythia Minor, Roman Empire (now Constanța, Romania).

Statue of Ovidius in Constanta, Romania. Ovidius, in 8 AD, suddenly was sent personally by Augustus, 71, into exile to Tomis (now Constanta, Romania) in the eastern province Scythila Minor, on the Black Sea, where he remained until his death in 17.

Ovidius was very popular, but, suddenly, was sent personally by Augustus, 71, into exile to Tomis (now Constanta, Romania) in the eastern province Scythila Minor, on the Black Sea, where he remained for 9 years, until his death in 17. Ovidius himself attributes his exile to *carmen et error*, "a poem and a mistake". It is not yet clear why Ovidius was banished, but, in my view, the reason is that Ovidius was close to Augustus's family, especially to grandson Agrippa Postumus, now 20 and exiled for antisocial behavior, to granddaughter Julia the Younger, 27, also banished (for having an affair with a senator), and to her husband Lucius Aemilius Paullus (37 BC – 8, aged 45), who was executed as a conspirator in a plot against Augustus – it seems that Ovidius new about the plot, but did not inform Augustus.

Banishment of Augustus's granddaughter Julia the Younger (19 BC – 29 in Isole Tremiti, aged 48), now 27, daughter of Agrippa and Augustus's daughter Julia the Elder (also banished).

2017 – 14 December – After 2009 years, Rome city council overturned banishment of 'one of the greatest poets', after Augustus forced him to leave on the year 8. Therefore, 2009 years after Augustus banished him to Tomis, on the Black Sea (now Constanța, Romania), the poet Ovidius has been rehabilitated.

Rome city council on Thursday, 14 Dec 2017, unanimously approved a motion tabled by the M5S party to "repair the serious wrong" suffered by Ovidius, thought of as one of the three canonical poets of Latin literature, along with Vergilius and Horatius.

Best known for his 15-book epic narrative poem Metamorphoses, and the elegy Ars Amatoria, or the Art of Love, Publius Ovidius Naso was exiled in 8 AD to Tomis, the ancient Black Sea settlement now known as the Romanian port city of Constanța.

He remained there until his death, about 9 years later. Although ordered directly by the emperor, scholars have long speculated over the motive for Ovidius' exile; the poet himself attributed it to "carmen et error", a poem and a mistake.

Experts believe the cause was probably a combination of three factors: that Ovidius' erotic poetry was considered offensive, his attitude to Augustus was too disrespectful, and that he may have been involved in an unspecified plot or scandal.

Rome's deputy mayor said: "It is about the fundamental right of artists to express themselves freely in societies in which, around the world, the freedom of artistic expression is increasingly constrained". Ovidius was indisputably "one of the greatest poets in the history of humanity," the deputy mayor said, and moreover the real reasons for his mysterious banishment by the emperor "were never placed on the historical record".

Sulmona, the Abruzzo town where the poet was born (then Sulmo), formally acquitted him of any wrongdoing. Dante Alighieri (30 May 1265, Firenze, Italy – 14 Sep 1321, Ravenna, Italy, aged 56.3), the great Renaissance poet, was similarly pardoned in 2008 by Firenze (Florence) – from where he was exiled on pain of death in 1302 (he was 37), 706 years ago.

1614. – Shakespeare was 50 when The Globe Theatre reopens.

9– Ovidius, 51, is in Tomis.

Publius Quinctilius Varus, Roman general and politician, born in 46 BC, dies at 55, in a battle in the Teutoburg Forest, 100 km northeast of current Dortmund, Germany.

Germany, 22 March 1978, Dortmund, the store Besta Hungshans (left), Avis rental service (center).

1615. - Shakespeare, 51, was probably sick.

10– Ovidius, 52, was in Tomis.

1616. – February – Shakespeare's daughter Judith married Thomas Quiney, a vintner. The Quineys had three children, all of whom died without marrying. The elder daughter Susanna Halls had one child, Elizabeth, who married twice, but died without children in 1670, ending Shakespeare's direct line.

25 March - Shakespeare signed his last will and testament.

22 April – death of Miguel de Cervantes (29 Sep 1547 – 22 April 1616, aged 68.4, the greatest writer in the Spanish language, and one of the world's best novelists).

23 April – William Shakespeare, 52, died on his birthday, April 23rd, in Stratford-upon-Avon, his burial being recorded in the Stratford Holy Church Register two days later. His grave is in the Holy Trinity Church, where his baptism was recorded 52 years ago.

1619. – Hamlet was performed as part of Christmas celebrations at the court of King James I (19 June 1566 – 27 March 1625, aged 58.7).

12: First consulship of Germanicus (15 BC – 19, aged 34, son of Tiberius's brother Nero Claudius Drusus and Antonia Minor, adopted by Tiberius), now 27. Birth of Caligula on August 31, as Gaius Julius Caesar Germanicus, son of Germanicus and Agrippina the Elder (15 BC – 33, aged 48, daughter of Julia the Elder (daughter of Augustus), buried in the Mausoleum of Augustus), grandson of Tiberius, great-grandson of Augustus, the 3rd Roman Emperor, after Tiberius, from 37 to 24 January 41, for a little more than 3 years, when he died at 28.4.

Rome, Forum Romanum (ruins of Palace of Caligula (left), Curia (Senate House (center)), Altare della Patria (back), from the Palatine Hill.

13: The Temple of Rome and Augustus is built at Ostia (20 km southwest of Rome, the harbor city of Rome; os means mouth in Latin). Tiberius's (54) tribunician and other powers are renewed for a further ten years, with authority equal to that of Augustus, 76, on 23 September.

Rome, Trajan's column (113, center-left), la Chiesa Santissimo Nome di Maria al Foro Traiano (center-right), both at the north-west end of Foro Traiano. The fragments of the columns were part of Basilica Ulpia, which was in the center of the Forum in 113 AD, south-est of the column. The East (Latin) Library was to the right (north-est) of the column, and the West (Greek) Library was to the left (south-est) of the column.

14: on 19 August Augustus died in Nola, Roman Empire (now in Italy), aged 75.9 (just 35 days before 76), being the first Roman emperor for 40 years and 7 months. Burial place: Mausoleum of Augustus in Rome. In the same year, his daughter Julia the Elder (known as Julia Caesaris filia or Julia Augusti filia), who had 3 husbands and 6 children, died, aged 53.

Tiberius (54.7) succeeds Augustus from 14 to 37 (23 years).

Augustus is deified on 17 September.

The reign of Augustus initiated an era of peace known as the Pax Romana (The Roman Peace). The Roman world was largely free from large-scale conflict for more than two centuries (there were continuous wars of imperial expansion on the Empire's frontiers, and the year-long civil war known as the "Year of the Four Emperors", in 69, over the imperial succession). Augustus dramatically enlarged the Empire, annexing Egypt, Dalmatia (Illyria or Illyricum, former Yugoslavia and Albania), Pannonia (parts of and around Austria, Hungary, north-western Yugoslavia), Noricum (parts of Austria and Slovenia), and Raetia (parts of Austria, Germany, Switzerland); expanding possessions in Africa; expanding into Germania; and completing the conquest of Hispania. Beyond the frontiers, he secured the Empire with a buffer region of client states, and made peace with the Parthian Empire (Iran, Iraq, and around) through diplomacy. He reformed the Roman system of taxation, developed networks of roads with an official courier system, established a standing army, established the Praetorian Guard, created official police and fire-fighting services for Rome, and rebuilt much of the city during his reign.

Statue of the Roman Emperor Trajan (53 – 117, emperor 98 – 117). Inscription under the statue: SPQR (Senatus Populusque Romanus) Imperatore Cesare Nerve Traiano, Optimo Principi. The Roman Empire reached its greatest territorial extent under Trajan, with conquests in Dacia, Arabia, Armenia, and Mesopotamia.

Aphorisms of Augustus

Festina lente - Make haste slowly.

Give me a safe commander, not a rash one.

I found Rome of clay; I leave it to you of marble.

Livia, ostri coniugii memor vive, ac vale - Livia, keep our marriage alive, and farewell.

Acta est fabula, plaudite! - The play is over, applaud! (The last words of the Roman Emperor Augustus)

Trajan's column (113, center-left), la Chiesa Santissimo Nome di Maria al Foro Traiano (center-right), both at the north-west end of Foro Traiano. The five fragments of columns (in front of the picture) were part of Basilica Ulpia, which was in the center of the Forum in 113 AD, south-est of the column. The East (Latin) Library was to the right (north-est) of the column, and the West (Greek) Library was to the left (south-est) of the column.

17– Publis Ovidius Naso died in Tomis, Moesia, Roman Empire (now Constanța, Romania), aged circa 59.

Ovidius' many poems and letters in exile, collected in Tristia and The Black Sea Letters, have been described by critics as a "clinical presentation" of the condition of exile, "demonstrating its debilitating effect upon a man's morale, his talents and perhaps his psychology".

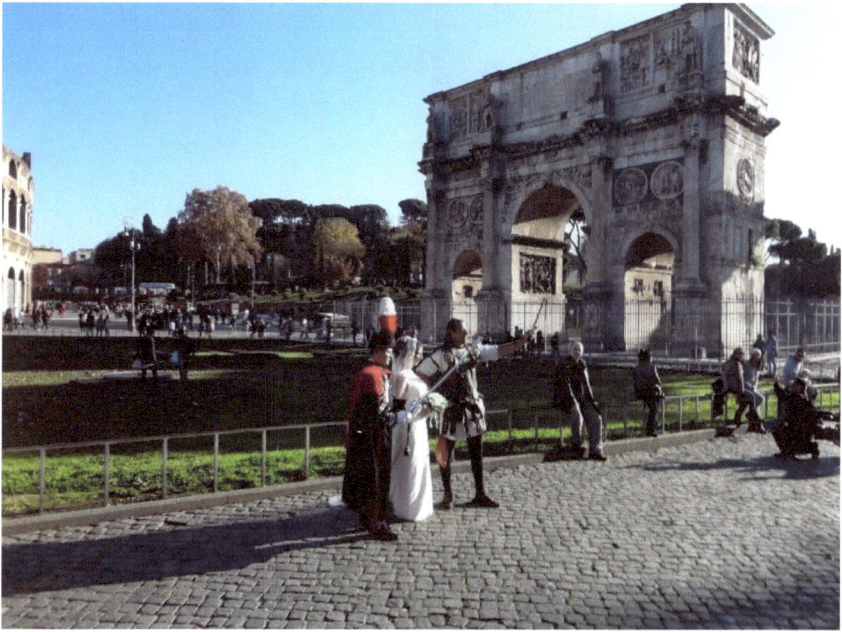

The Amphitheatrum Flavium (Colosseum, 80 AD, left), the Arch of Constantine (315 AD, right) and a carabiniere wedding photo event.

Constanta, Romania, Piazza Ovidiu: Statue of Publius Ovidius Naso (20 March 43 BC, in Sulmona – 17, in Tomis, Moesia (now Constanta, Romania), aged circa 59.

1622. – 15 January - birth of Molière (15 Jan 1622 – 17 Feb 1673, aged 51.1, full name Jean-Baptiste Poquelin, known by his stage name Molière, a French playwright, actor and poet).

1623. – Shakespeare's wife, Anne (1556 - 1623, aged 67) died.

Fellow actors John Heminges, 67, (25 Nov 1556 – 10 Oct 1630, aged 73.9) and Henry Condell, 47, (1576 – Dec 1627, aged 51) gather together and publish for the first time, 7 years after the death of Shakespeare, 36 of Shakespeare's circa 39 plays, in a collection known as The First Folio.

Blaise Pascal was born (1623 – 1662, aged 39), French mathematician, physicist, philosopher and writer.

William Shakespeare is the best-selling fiction author of all time (estimated 4 billions of copies sold).

Chapter 3. Dialog about Pythagoras

This chapter is written in the form of a dialog between me and an imaginary person representing The Sun, because The Sun is the only one which observed the Earth from its creation until now, and the life on Earth would not be possible without The Sun.

DEDIU

Your Majesty The Sun,

THE SUN

My friend, I appreciate your politeness, which is so desirable, but often missing, on Earth, with only few using it, but, for this book, please call me Mr. Sun.

DEDIU

Mr. Sun, please tell me about Pythagoras and others.

THE SUN

Pythagoras and Vergilius have a great importance for your current civilization on Earth, which started over 2800 years ago with Homer, who was born around 850 BC and died around 780 BC (I know exactly the dates, but I let your specialists on Earth the pleasure to discover them). He was a great ancient Greek epic poet of the Odyssey and Iliad.

DEDIU

What about the ancient Egyptians and Chinese?

THE SUN

They both had remarkable civilizations, and some of them revered me as a God, which shows that they understood my importance, but, unfortunately, besides the pyramids and other important monuments, they did not leave too many elements of advanced civilization to be used to this day.

DEDIU

And Homer?

THE SUN

Look at some of his quotations:

For rarely are sons similar to their fathers: most are worse, and a few are better than their fathers.

In youth and beauty, wisdom is but rare!

There is nothing nobler or more admirable than when a man and a woman, who see eye to eye, keep house as man and wife, confounding their enemies and delighting their friends.

DEDIU
All are very true and eternal!
THE SUN
Yes, indeed. After Homer, another remarkable personality is Solon, 638 BC - 558 BC, an Athenian statesman and poet, whom I liked much, about 2600 years ago.
DEDIU
Why?
THE SUN
It is rare to see a statesman who is also a poet. Look at some of his quotes:

Laws are the spider's webs which, if anything small falls into them they ensnare it, but large things break through and escape.

I grow old learning something new every day.

Learn to obey before you command.

Put more trust in nobility of character than in an oath.

In giving advice seek to help, not to please, your friend.

DEDIU
Very inspiring.
THE SUN

Yes, and very useful every day. Now, one more precursor of Pythagoras: Aesop, 620 BC – 560 BC, an ancient Greek fabulist.
DEDIU

The first fabulist.
THE SUN

Yes. And the best. Here are some of his quotes.

Better be wise by the misfortunes of others than by your own.

In critical moments even the very powerful have need of the weakest.

It is thrifty to prepare today for the wants of tomorrow.

Injuries may be forgiven, but not forgotten.

It is easy to be brave from a safe distance.

United we stand, divided we fall.

DEDIU

One better than another. Let's also remember the first true mathematician and philosopher - Thales of Miletus (ca. 624 BC – 547 BC, age 77), 54 years older than Pythagoras, and Thales died when Pythagoras was 23. Thales' theorem, which states that if A, B and C are points on a circle, where the line AC is a diameter of the circle, then the angle ABC is a right angle. Also Anaximenes of Miletus, (585 BC - 528 BC, age 57), 15 years older than Pythagoras (Anaximenes died when Pythagoras was 42), was a Greek philosopher and mathematician.
THE SUN

That's right. Now let's focus on Pythagoras, ca. 570 BC – ca. 490 BC. He lived about 80 years, and he is also called Pythagoras of Samos.
DEDIU

He was a great Ionian Greek mathematician and philosopher.
THE SUN

Not only that, he had, and continue to have an important influence on Earth. For example this quotation:

Were it not for number and its nature, nothing that exists would be clear to anybody either in itself or in its relation to other things...You can observe the power of number exercising itself ... in all acts and the thoughts of men, in all handicrafts and music.

DEDIU

Here we have very clearly expressed the fundamental role of the number.

THE SUN

Without numbers nothing could be quantified, explained and built.

DEDIU

Not even music would exist without numbers.

THE SUN

Another quote:

A thought is an idea in transit.

DEDIU

What a beautiful quote!

THE SUN

And very profound too. Another one:

Do not talk a little on many subjects, but much on a few.

DEDIU

This quote shows that from Pythagoras comes the idea of specialization, which so important today.

THE SUN

Yes, and also the idea of interdisciplinary collaboration, because he refers to "a few" not just one. What about this one?

The oldest, shortest words - "yes" and "no" - are those which require the most thought.

DEDIU

This quote is not only very true, but is also the beginning of the binary algebra, which uses the numbers 1 and 0, 1 for yes, we have electrical contact, and 0 for no, there is no electrical circuit. Today all the computers and many related devices use this binary algebra.

THE SUN

You see, all started with Pythagoras! Listen to this one:

Silence is better than unmeaning words.

DEDIU

Oh, this silence is so precious and impossible to find.

THE SUN

Right. It is outrageous that some governments require some companies, like the railroads companies, to make as much noise as they can at crossroads, to make people sick. Somebody there on Earth will have to stop these unhealthy practices.

DEDIU

The sooner the better.

THE SUN

Yes, and Pythagoras' quote is so necessary these days, when mediocrity dictates, and talks continuously. I like these clear ideas. Now we have this quote:

Reason is immortal, all else mortal.

DEDIU

This importance given to reason is really remarkable.

THE SUN

No doubt about that. And now a very strong quote:

As soon as laws are necessary for men, they are no longer fit for freedom.

DEDIU

This quote makes you thing very seriously.

THE SUN

Yes, in general they say that freedom is obeying the laws, but Pythagoras insists that if laws are necessary for men, it means that the men cannot control themselves, and the government has to force them to obey some laws, therefore these men are no longer fit

for freedom. Obviously, wise men do not need laws, they understand each other, and they solve their differences in a calm and harmonious manner.
DEDIU
Exactly.
THE SUN
Now a quote which I like because of the star.

Above the cloud with its shadow is the star with its light. Above all things reverence thyself.

DEDIU
Yes, he worked much on astronomy and created the word kosmos.
THE SUN
Let's see another great quote:

Concern should drive us into action, and not into a depression. No man is free, who cannot control himself.

DEDIU
It is so powerful and clear! Self-control was one of the most important Pythagorean principles.
THE SUN
A quote about body and soul:

Choose rather to be strong of soul than strong of body.

DEDIU
Yes, Pythagoras, being a believer of metempsychosis, separated the soul (which he said that is a combination of life-principles, self and mind) from the body, which was considered as a container, or prison. In his view the soul was immortal, a kind of fallen divinity, and transmigrated from one body to another.
THE SUN
Another beautiful quote:

Rest satisfied with doing well, and leave others to talk of you as they will.

DEDIU

Excellent quote. It is certain that Pythagoras had a very good communication between the left and right hemispheres of his brain, because this is required for mathematical ability. A recent study, that used functional magnetic resonance imaging to measure brain activity, showed that the strength of communication between the left and right hemispheres of the brain predicts performance on basic arithmetic problems. The results explain the neural basis of human mathematical abilities, and suggest a possible medical treatment for those who suffer from dyscalculia—an inability to understand and work with numbers.

THE SUN

Very interesting. Pythagoras would have certainly liked mathematical modeling. Any news?

DEDIU

Yes, and you are involved too, as always. You know, solar panels, like those commonly perched atop house roofs or in sunny fields, quietly harvesting your radiant energy, are useful, but they could be better, especially more efficient, durable, and affordable. Many specialists are working on these issues, using some nanotechnology, and a lot of mathematical modeling.

THE SUN

I like this. Let's have a new quote:

Strength of mind rests in sobriety; for this keeps your reason unclouded by passion.

DEDIU

Indeed, passion and strength of mind do not go together.

THE SUN

A quote about geometry:

There is geometry in the humming of the strings, there is music in the spacing of the spheres.

DEDIU

Very elegant, indeed. Pythagoras was first to observe that the pitch of a musical note is proportional to the geometrical length of the string that produced it, and that intervals between harmonious sound frequencies form certain numerical ratios. He suggested that you, the Sun, Moon and planets emit their unique hum based on their orbital revolutions, and this is the music in the spacing of the spheres.

THE SUN

He is certainly right, and there are many more facts for you on Earth to discover. What is the situation with Voyager?

DEDIU

Voyager 1 was launched to Jupiter and Saturn on September 5, 1977, and 35 years after leaving Earth, in 2012, is close to the boundary that separates the Solar System and interstellar space. The Solar System is enveloped in a big plasma bubble. This hot and turbulent region is created by a stream of charged particles from you, the Sun. Outside the plasma bubble is the space between stars in the Milky Way. Together with Voyager 2, which was launched two weeks earlier, they are the longest operating spacecraft in history and the most distant, in different directions. In 2012 Voyager 1 was more than 17 billion miles from you, the Sun, and Voyager 2 more than 14 billion miles from you.

THE SUN

I see, they run away....

DEDIU

Not really, nothing personal, just scientific experiment. They still work, even if each only has 68 KB of computer memory, which is about 100,000 times less than a small computer from 2012. Each also has an eight-track tape recorder, while in 2012 the spacecraft use digital memory.

THE SUN

What was their original goal?

DEDIU

The Voyagers' original goal was to tour Jupiter and Saturn, and they sent back pictures of Jupiter's big red spot, and Saturn's reflecting rings. They also sent to Earth many discoveries: erupting volcanoes on the Jupiter moon Io; hints of an ocean below the icy surface of Europa, another Jupiter moon; signs of methane rain on the Saturn moon Titan. Voyager 2 then journeyed to Uranus and Neptune. It remains the only spacecraft to fly by these two outer planets. Voyager 1 used Saturn as a gravitational slingshot to catapult itself toward the boundary of the solar system.

THE SUN

What fuel do they use?

DEDIU

They use nuclear power, are about the size of a 2012 subcompact car, and still have five instruments to study magnetic fields, cosmic rays and charged particles from you, known as solar wind. They also carry gold-plated discs containing multilingual greetings, music and pictures — in the small chance that other intelligent species will find them. Since 2004, Voyager 1 has been exploring a region in the bubble at the solar system's edge where the solar wind dramatically slows and heats up. Over the last several months of 2012, scientists have seen changes that suggest Voyager 1 is on the verge of crossing over. The spacecraft has enough fuel to last until around 2020. By that time, probably Voyager will already be moving between the stars of the Milky Way.

THE SUN

Impressive progress from Pythagoras until 2012. Any news about the radiation belts surrounding Earth?

DEDIU

On August 30, 2012, it was launched from Cape Canaveral the racket Atlas V, with the twin Radiation Belt Storm Probes (RBSP). There are five instruments aboard the RBSP. One of them is the space weather instrument RBSP Ion Composition Experiment known as RBSPICE. Each RBSP spacecraft weighs about 660 kilograms and carries an identical set of five instrument suites that will examine the radiation belts surrounding Earth.

THE SUN

Pythagoras would be really delighted to see these achievements. Here is another quote:

It is better wither to be silent, or to say things of more value than silence. Sooner throw a pearl at hazard than an idle or useless word; and do not say a little in many words, but a great deal in a few.

DEDIU

Silence was very important for Pythagoras, and he insisted on this issue, as we can see.

THE SUN

As I can see from here, today, unfortunately, the noise is the dominant factor everywhere, especially in the form of idle and useless words. The mediocretization of the society is progressing dangerously fast. Well, maybe the things will change in better. Now this quote.

Virtue is harmony.

DEDIU

Virtue is so important and so beneficial, that, indeed, creates a harmony.

THE SUN

Beautiful, undeniably. Now let's discuss some other details. Tell me something about Samos.

DEDIU

Pythagoras of Samos was born on the Samos island, which is a Greek island in the eastern Aegean Sea, just 1.6 km from the coast of Asia Minor, where is Turkey, about 250 km East of Athens, and 350 km North-East of Crete.

THE SUN

Who else was born on this island?

DEDIU

Epicurus, another famous philosopher, and the astronomer Aristarchus of Samos, who was the first astronomer to suggest that the Earth revolves around you, The Sun, and not vice-versa.

THE SUN

Don't say! Nice to hear that again. I remember sending Aristarchus a special ray, when he suggested this fact. Was Pythagoras married?

DEDIU

Yes, with Theano, and they had four children: Damo, Myia, Telauges and Arignote. Pythagoras' mother was Pythais, and father Mnesarchus, a merchant who came from Tyre.

THE SUN

Nice family, I remember them. And, after about 80 years of great achievements, knowing that his reason is immortal, where did he pass to eternity in 490 BC?

DEDIU

Far from his Samos, at Metapontum, which was an important ancient Greek city of Magna Graecia, currently in the Southern Italy, on the gulf of Tarentum, about 140 km east of Napoli (Naples), and 160 km northeast of Messina, Sicilia (Sicily).

THE SUN

You are a mathematician; tell me more about Pythagoras as a mathematician.

DEDIU

Pythagoras is the first pure mathematician, and has a fundamental role in the development of mathematics. In his time, a big problem was the duplication of the square, and this gave rise to the famous Pythagorean Theorem or Pythagoras' theorem:

In any right triangle, the area of the square on the hypotenuse (opposite the right angle) is equal to the sum of the areas of the squares on the other two sides of the triangle.

THE SUN

Where did Pythagoras work?

DEDIU

As a child Pythagoras travelled with his father, who was a merchant, to Babylonia, Phoenicia and Egypt, then around 530 BC, when he was forty, because of a tyrannical ruler, he moved to the city of Croton, a Dorian Greek colony in southern Italy, about 30 km northeast of Metapontum. There he lectured in philosophy and mathematics, and he founded an academy, gradually transformed in a society called Order of the Pythagoreans, which was, at the same time, a scientific school and a religious community. Here are the roots of later monastic orders.

THE SUN

Any degrees of membership for Pythagoreans?

DEDIU

Three:

1) novices or Politics, that is Politics don't know much;
2) first degree of initiation, or Nomothets;

3) Mathematicians, or experts.

THE SUN

I see, starting from that time the mathematicians are the experts. Any connection with Anaximander?

DEDIU

Pythagoras was a disciple of Anaximander, who was an astronomer, and Pythagoras developed Anaximander' cosmical system. Aristotle writes about these developments.

THE SUN

What did Pythagoras write?

DEDIU

Nothing, because of the pledge of secrecy, but later he was considered as a semi-divine man, who originated many important ideas. This glorification of Pythagoras shows his immense influence on our civilization, as a mathematician, scientist and philosopher.

THE SUN

Was Pythagoras famous in his own day?

DEDIU

Yes, and even 150 years later, in the time of Plato and Aristotle. His fame was mostly from a religious point of view, because he was the founder of a religion, Pythagoreanism, with many devoted followers, based on a strict way of life, with rigorous self-discipline, religious ritual, dietary restrictions, hardworking, and the believe that the soul was immortal and went through many reincarnations. On this idea Plato's doctrine of Recollection is based.

THE SUN

The famous general George Patton believed in reincarnation, therefore he was a follower of Pythagoras. Even today there are many followers of Pythagoras. Other achievements of Pythagoras?

DEDIU

He had great influence in music and medicine. Pythagoras discovered the numerical ratios, which determine the concordant intervals of the musical scale. Plato writes about the fact that Pythagoras wanted the body to be strung like an instrument to a certain pitch. Musical tuning and health appear from the application of Limit to the Unlimited, which idea is the main contribution of Pythagoras to philosophy. The main achievement is that he had many followers for over 2500 years, and they all believe that the numbers are very important in all activities.

THE SUN

It seems that everybody agrees with this Pythagorean idea. And Pythagoras would have liked the advanced research of these days. Any example?

DEDIU

Yes, for instance simulating the birth of a planet. Over the past several decades, the search for extrasolar planets has yielded many discoveries. Now, planetary researchers have a new tool - simulated model of how planets are born. A team of researchers are using supercomputers to model and simulate the protostellar disks that precede the formation of planets.

THE SUN

Interesting. I see that there good studies of me too.

DEDIU

Of course. From the interior of the Sun, to the upper atmosphere and near-space environment of Earth, and outwards to a region far beyond Pluto where the Sun's influence wanes, advances during the past decade in space physics and solar physics have yielded important insights into the phenomena that affect the space station. There is a program of basic and applied research for 10 years that will advance scientific understanding of the Sun, Sun-Earth connections and the origins of "space weather," and the Sun's interactions with other bodies in the solar system. There are many questions in planetary science that need to be answered.

THE SUN

Beautiful. Any mathematical news?

DEDIU

Yes, like computing with water droplets and superhydrophobic materials. Researchers have experimentally determined the conditions for rebounding of water droplets moving on superhydrophobic surfaces. Similar to billiard balls, these droplets move by way of collisions, allowing the scientists to build a droplet logic. When combined with chemical reactions these devices demonstrate elementary Boolean logic operations. There is also an effort by mathematicians to offer a unified theory of dark matter and dark energy. It has been proposed a unified theory of dark matter and dark energy that alters the equations describing the fundamentals of gravity. The mathematicians suggest the law of energy and momentum conservation in space-time is valid only when normal matter, dark matter, and dark energy are all taken into account.

THE SUN

Now let's go back to Pythagoras and give us more details about his mathematical accomplishments.

DEDIU

In addition to the Pythagorean Theorem, Pythagoras and his followers were interested in the principles of mathematics, the concept of mathematical figures, and the idea of a proof. They wanted to understand more deeply the fundamental ideas, and, as it were customary at that time, they though that there is something divine in all this process. Therefore there was some combination of mathematics and theology in the Pythagoreans' geometry, arithmetic, astronomy, and music.

THE SUN

And what did Aristotle say about Pythagoras?

DEDIU

Here are some quotations from Aristotle:

(The Pythagoreans) both hold that the infinite is being, and divide it. And the Pythagoreans say that there is a void, and that it enters into the heaven itself from the infinite air, as though it (the heaven) were breathing; and this void defines the natures of things, inasmuch as it is a certain separation and definition of things that lie and this is true first in the case of numbers, for the void defines the nature of these.

Some think it necessary that noise should arise when so great bodies are in motion, since sound does arise from bodies among us, which are not so large and do not move so swiftly; and from the Sun and Moon, and from the stars in so great number, and of so great size, moving so swiftly, there must necessarily arise a sound inconceivably great. Assuming these things, and that the swiftness has the principle of harmony by reason of the intervals, they say that the sound of the stars moving on in a circle becomes musical. And since it seems unreasonable that we also do not hear this sound, they say that the reason for this is that the noise exists in the very nature of things, so as not to be distinguishable from the opposite silence; for the distinction of sound and silence lies in their contrast with each other, so that as blacksmiths think there is no difference between them, because they are accustomed to the sound, so the same thing happens to men.

They say that the whole heaven is limited, the opposite to what those of Italy, called the Pythagoreans, say; for these say that fire is at the center, and that the earth is one of the stars, and that moving in a circle about the center it produces night and day. And they assume yet another earth opposite this, which they call the counter-earth, not seeking reasons and causes for phenomena, but stretching phenomena to meet certain assumptions and opinions of theirs, and attempting to arrange them in a system. . . .

And farther the Pythagoreans say that the most authoritative part of the All stands guard, because it is specially fitting that it should, and this part is the center; and this place that the fire occupies, they call the guard of Zeus, as it is called simply the center, that is, the center of space and the center of matter and of nature.

The same holds true for those who construct the heaven out of numbers; for some construct nature out of numbers, as do certain of the Pythagoreans.

With these and before them (Anaxagoras, Empedokles, Atomists) those called Pythagoreans applying themselves to the sciences, first developed them; and being brought up in them they thought that the first principles of these (i.e. numbers) were the first principles of all things. And since of these (sciences) numbers are by nature the first, in numbers rather than in fire and earth and water they thought they saw many likenesses to things that are and that are coming to be, as, for instance, justice is such a property of numbers, and soul and mind are such a property, and another is opportunity, and of other things one may say the same of each one.

And further, discerning in numbers the conditions and reasons of harmonies also; since, moreover, other things seemed to be like numbers in their entire nature, and numbers were the first of every nature, they assumed that the elements of numbers were the elements of all things, and that the whole heavens were harmony and number. And whatever characteristics in numbers and harmonics they could show were in agreement with the properties of the heavens and its parts, and with its whole arrangement, these they collected and adapted; and if there chanced to be any gap anywhere, they eagerly sought that the whole system might be connected with these (stray phenomena). To give an example of my meaning: inasmuch as ten seemed to be the perfect number and to embrace the whole nature of numbers, they asserted that the number of bodies moving through the heavens were ten, and when only nine were visible, for the reason just stated they postulated the counter-earth as the tenth. We have given a more definite account of these thinkers in other parts of our writings. But we have referred to them here with this purpose in view, that we might ascertain from them what they asserted as the first principles, and in what manner they came upon the causes that have been enumerated. They certainly seem to consider number as the first principle, and as it were the matter in things and in their conditions and states; and the odd and the even are elements of number, and of these the one is infinite and the other finite, and unity is the product of both of them, for it is both odd and even, and number arises from unity, and the whole heaven, as has been said, is numbers.

And Plato only changed the name, for the Pythagoreans say that things exist by imitation of numbers, but Plato, by sharing the nature of numbers.

The thinkers known as the Pythagoreans were the first to pursue mathematical studies and advance them.

THE SUN

It is clear that Pythagoras was the first to see the importance of the numbers and mathematics in the universe.

DEDIU

Yes, the Pythagoreans discovered many ideas, such as the five regular solids, the Pythagorean Theorem, and the existence of irrational numbers. Thus, by searching for the truth and universal harmony through mathematics, the Pythagoreans made many important discoveries in different areas of mathematics and science that are both mathematically rigorous, and continue to be applied today.

THE SUN

What about astronomy?

DEDIU

The Pythagoreans made numerous findings in the field of astronomy that are remarkably accurate, considering the lack of observational instruments in their day. For example, they hypothesized that the earth is round by observing the shadow of the earth on the moon during a lunar eclipse. Also, they believed that you, the Sun, and other planets are spheres as well, and that they orbited in a circular motion. The Pythagoreans noticed that the orbit of the moon was tilted to the equatorial plane of the Earth, and that both the morning and evening star were the planet Venus. They believed in harmony, and the basic principle of a mathematically ordered universe is a numerical proportion.

THE SUN

Where is the music?

DEDIU

The Pythagoreans believed that the planets produced sounds while orbiting in the universe, producing a harmony of the spheres. In this way Pythagoras' work on music and music theory starts. Another great discovery of Pythagoras is that musical intervals may be reduced to numerical ratios. He discovered three musical intervals, the fourth, the fifth, and the octave, by experimenting with the monochord, a one-stringed instrument with a moveable bridge. Pythagoras observed that vibrating strings produce harmonious sounds when the ratios of the lengths of the strings are whole numbers. Specifically, the ratio of the octave is 1:2; the perfect fifth, 2:3; the perfect fourth, 3:4. This mathematical and musical discovery is interconnected by the Pythagoreans to the universe itself; they considered the universe to be composed of numbers and thus concluded that the ratios that Pythagoras discovered in music were also present in the relations of celestial bodies to one another. They applied the newfound ratios to the harmonious sounds that the planets supposedly produce. As we can see, this is another instance of applying mathematics to the universe. The discovery of musical intervals was the foundation of music theory, and continues to be relevant.

THE SUN

Let's return to the numbers, which rule the universe, as Pythagoras said.

DEDIU

Pythagoras' use of numbers was a search for truth and configurations in the universe. The Pythagoreans were the first to use numerical and geometrical illustrations as models of cosmic order. The five regular solids (which are the only solids that have all edges and all interior angles equal) they discover are: cube, tetrahedron, octahedron, dodecahedron, and icosahedron. The Pythagoreans also undertook the idea of geometric dimensions. One represented the point, two represented the line, three represented the plane, and four was the tetrahedron, the first three-dimensional object. They proved that the sum of the interior angles of a triangle is equal to 180 degrees. The Pythagoreans discovered the existence of irrational numbers. To see the importance of numbers in everything, we have this recent example: looking for the smallest ice crystals in the world, an imaginative experiment has recently revealed the minimum number of molecules needed before water forms a crystalline structure. It was previously thought that around 1,000 molecules were the minimum necessary for a complete crystal, but now crystal formation can be detected from as little as 275 molecules.

THE SUN

Nice example. Tell me about the mathematics of leaf decay.

DEDIU

The natural decay of organic carbon contributes more than 90% of the yearly carbon dioxide released into Earth's atmosphere and oceans. Understanding the rate at which leaves decay can help scientists predict this global flux of carbon dioxide. But a single leaf may undergo different rates of decay, depending on many variables. Researchers have just built a mathematical model that incorporates these variables, and have discovered a common element within the diversity of leaf decay.

THE SUN

Mathematics and numbers are everywhere. Who are some important contemporaries of Pythagoras?

DEDIU

About 7 years younger than Pythagoras was Gautama Buddha, 563 BC – 483 BC, Indian Founder of Buddhism. Here are some of his quotes:

All wrong-doing arises because of mind. If mind is transformed can wrong-doing remain?

Better than a thousand hollow words, is one word that brings peace.

Holding on to anger is like grasping a hot coal with the intent of throwing it at someone else; you are the one who gets burned

About 19 years younger was Confucius, 551 BC – 479 BC, Chinese philosopher, teacher, politician and editor. His quotes:

Do not impose on others what you yourself do not desire.

When a country is governed well, poverty and mean condition are things to be ashamed of. When a country is governed poorly, riches and honor are things to be ashamed of.

He acts before he speaks, and afterwards speaks according to his actions.

The mind of the superior man is conversant with virtue; the mind of the base man is conversant with gain.

About 35 years younger was another Greek philosopher Heraclitus, 535 BC – 475 BC, who said:

The only constant is change.

No man ever steps in the same river twice, for it's not the same river and he's not the same man.

A man's character is his guardian divinity.

Change alone is unchanging.

Good character is not formed in a week or a month. It is created little by little, day by day. Protracted and patient effort is needed to develop good character.

About 45 years younger was Aeschylus, 525 BC – 456 BC, ancient Greek playwright, father of tragedy. His quotes:

I'm not afraid of storms, for I'm learning to sail my ship.

By polluting clear water with slime you will never find good drinking water.

By Time and Age full many things are taught.

Everyone's quick to blame the alien.

The west side, with the main entrance, of Mount Washington Resort, Bretton Woods, New Hampshire, USA, where the United Nations Monetary and Financial Conference took place in July 1944.

Chapter 4. Dialog about Plato

THE SUN

Let's discuss now about Plato. But first who other important personalities are between Pythagoras and Plato?

DEDIU

About 74 years younger than Pythagoras was Sophocles, 496 BC – 406 BC, ancient Greek playwright. Sophocles was a cute 6 years old boy when Pythagoras passed to the eternity.

Number of years after the passing of Pythagoras:
- 6 – Herodotus, 484 BC – 425 BC, Greek historian
- 21 – Socrates, 469 BC – 399 BC, Greek Athenian philosopher
- 30 – Democritus, 460 BC – 370 BC, Greek Athenian philosopher
- 30 – Hippocrates, 460 BC – 375 BC, Greek physician, the father of medicine
- 30 – Thucydides, 460 BC – 395 BC, Greek historian and author

Then, about 63 years after the passing of Pythagoras, we have Plato, 427 BC – 347 BC, a very important classical Greek philosopher, mathematician and writer.

THE SUN

Where was Plato born?

DEDIU

Plato was born in Athens, in 427 BC, his father being Ariston. Plato's grandfather, from the father side, was Aristokles, who was a direct descendant of Solon's brother Exekestiades. Solon, 638 BC - 558 BC, an Athenian statesman and poet, died 131 years before the birth of Plato. Plato's mother was Periktione, who was a sister of Charmides and cousin of Kritias. Plato had two brothers and a sister. The Great Peloponnesian War (Part I) started 4 years before his birth, and finished when he was 6. Young Plato received a musical and gymnastic education, and he wrote some juvenile epigrams and tragedies, but burned them once he became associated with Socrates, who was 42 years older. When Plato was 11 the Great Peloponnesian War (Part II) started, and ended when he was 16. At that time he became politically active. When Plato was 23 Athens lost the war to Sparta, and his uncle and cousin were among the Thirty Tyrants, who terrorized the Athenian state after that.

THE SUN

Was Plato present at the trial of Socrates?

DEDIU

Yes, Plato was 28, Socrates 70, but Plato was not allowed to speak. After the execution of Socrates, Plato and other disciples of Socrates moved to Megara, about 30 km west of Athens. There they created a Megarean School of Socratic philosophy, where Elkleides of Megara was well known. At this time, the first period of Plato's writing activity starts, until he was 37.

THE SUN

Did Plato serve in the military?

DEDIU

Yes, twice, when he was 32 and 33, probably in the Corinthian war.

THE SUN

And when did Plato come in contact with Pythagoreanism?

DEDIU

When he was 37, exactly 100 years after the passing of Pythagoras, Plato went in his first journey to Sicily and Italy, until he was 39. At that time Pythagoreanism was undergoing a renaissance in South Italy, under the leadership of Archytas of Tarentum, a well-known Pythagorean statesman and thinker. Plato visited several Pythagoreans in Southern Italy, one of whom, Theodorus, is also mentioned as a friend to Socrates in Plato's Theaetetus.

THE SUN

Tell me more about Plato's Theaetetus.

DEDIU

The Theaetetus is one of Plato's dialogues, written when Plato was 67 (and 9 years after the death of Theaetetus), in which the focus is on knowledge. The persons of the dialogue, which took place 39 years before, when Plato was 28, are the philosopher Socrates (age 70), and two mathematicians: Theodorus of Cyrene (ca 60, Pythagorean) and Theaetetus (age 18, student of Theodorus). They discuss three definitions of knowledge: knowledge as perception, knowledge as true judgment, and, knowledge as a true judgment with an account. Each of these definitions is shown to be inadequate. The conversation ends with Socrates' announcement that he has to go to court to answer to some charges.

THE SUN

What about the mathematician Theaetetus?

DEDIU

Theaetetus of Athens (ca. 417 BC – 369 BC) was 10 years younger than Plato and died at 48, apparently from wounds and dysentery on his way home, after fighting in an Athenian battle at Corinth, and his father probably was Euphronius. Theaetetus was a classical Greek mathematician, who has a crater on the Moon named after him. Some of his principal contributions were on irrational lengths, which were included, 70 years later, in *Book X* of Euclid's Elements (which has 13 books), and proving that there are exactly five regular convex polyhedra. Theaetetus, like Plato, was a student of the Greek mathematician Theodorus of Cyrene. Cyrene is in Libya, on the eastern end of the Gulf of Sidra. Theodorus had worked on incommensurable quantities, and Theaetetus continued those studies; classifying various forms of irrational numbers according to the way they are expressed as square roots.

THE SUN

Now back to Plato and Pythagoreanism.

DEDIU

In the Plato's Phaedo, there is Echecrates, another Pythagorean, in the group around Socrates, on his final day in prison. Plato's Pythagorean influences are quite evident in his interest in mathematics, and in some of his political ideals, expressed in various ways in several dialogues. Plato also had a first acquaintance with Dion of Syracuse, brother-in-law of Dionysius I, and with the young Dionysius II, who became tyrant 21 years later, in 367 BC, on the death of his father. Plato departed to Aegina, an island 37 km south-west of Athens, on orders of Dionysius I.

THE SUN

And the foundation of the Academy?

DEDIU

When Plato was 42 he founded the Academy, the first organized school, which became the model for other schools of higher learning, and later for European universities. The most famous student of Plato's Academy was Aristotle, 43 years younger.

Until the age of 60, Plato had his second period of writing activity. At the age of 61- 62, Plato had his second journey to Sicily. The *Sophistes* and the *Politicus* were written at the age of 62 – 66. The third Journey to Sicily, on the invitation of Dion, took place when Plato was 66 – 67. He was forced to live outside the palace, at the camp of the mercenaries. Dion wanted revolution, but Plato refused to participate. With the intervention of Archytas of Tarentum, Plato is allowed to return to Athens, in the summer of 360 BC, at the age of 67. After that, until his passing at the age of 80, Plato has his last period of writing activity.

THE SUN

Now let's discuss some of Plato's quotations.

DEDIU

Access to power must be confined to those who are not in love with it.

THE SUN

In order to implement this excellent quotation, it is necessary to have someone to control the access to power. Ideally the people should have this control, and, without any campaigning, they should elect the right people, not those who have campaigning money and agility.

DEDIU

Necessity is the mother of invention.

THE SUN

Necessity has many levels, from very acute, to almost invisible. At the acute level, the inventions respond direct and fast, but at the invisible level, many times the inventors come first with interesting products, which then become a necessity. For example the smartphones were not a stringent necessity, but slowly the people began to feel that they need them.

DEDIU

The worst of all deceptions is self-deception.

THE SUN

And it is very bad, indeed, when a big number of people suffer from a self-deception, in which case wars, or other damaging activities, may begin.

DEDIU

The penalty that good men pay for not being interested in politics is to be governed by men worse than themselves.

THE SUN

This is a heavy penalty indeed. Good people, many times, are not interested in politics, and the people should have the possibility to elect such good non-politicians, who will certainly have much better ideas for governing than the perpetual politicians, who reelect themselves for life.

DEDIU

Any man may easily do harm, but not every man can do good to another.

THE SUN

This is a law of the human society, and a lot of effort is needed to try to avoid the bad effects of this law. The most efficient are a good education and a good medical treatment. The legal system and the prisons are not efficient.

DEDIU

Every heart sings a song, incomplete, until another heart whispers back.

THE SUN

This is a very nice description of the law of attraction and love between a man and a woman, with the purpose of having children.

DEDIU

How can you prove whether at this moment we are sleeping, and all our thoughts are a dream; or whether we are awake, and talking to one another in the waking state?

THE SUN

An elegant description of the two fundamental philosophical ideas: idealism and materialism. Idealism means that all we see around is the result of our ideas and imagination. Materialism means that everything exists independent of our ideas. It is not yet clear which one is right.

DEDIU

The human behavior flows from three main sources: desire, emotion, and knowledge

THE SUN

And, of course, the behavior based on knowledge should be the dominant one and should control the desire and emotion.

DEDIU

I exhort you also to take part in the great combat, which is the combat of life, and greater than every other earthly conflict.
THE SUN

Everybody, volens nolens, takes part in the great combat of life, especially in the combat between a person and the millions of microbes, viruses, bacteria and many other permanent threats to a person's life. Plato refers mostly to the combat with other people for a better status in a society.
DEDIU

The excessive increase of anything causes a reaction in the opposite direction.
THE SUN

This is a general rule of the nature and of the human society, and it is important to be known and understood by everybody.
DEDIU

There are two things a person should never be angry at, what they can help, and what they cannot.
THE SUN

Because everything can be either helped or not helped, Plato implies that no one should ever be angry, which is an excellent advice.
DEDIU

Thinking: is the talking of the soul with itself.
THE SUN

This is a nice description of a complex brain process, in which the brain kind of talks with itself.
DEDIU

Those who wish to sing always find a song.
THE SUN

This quote has a great dose of symbolism, because Plato implies that if somebody wants to do something, then that person should find a way to do it.
DEDIU

Those who intend on becoming great should love neither themselves nor their own things, but only what is just, whether it happens to be done by themselves or others.
THE SUN

What a nice and clear description of a general rule for becoming great! Unfortunately, very few know or apply this just rule.

DEDIU

A hero is born among a hundred, a wise man is found among a thousand, but an accomplished one might not be found even among a hundred thousand men.

THE SUN

Let's see now some recent research.

DEDIU

Yes, experts in solar physics, climate models, paleoclimatology, and atmospheric science recently analyzed the Sun's variability over time and potential Sun-climate connections.

The effects of solar variability on Earth's climate are an important area of research, including the measurement record from space, and potential perturbations of climate due to long-term solar variability.

THE SUN

I certainly like this, and many interesting results will be found. Now back to Plato and the human soul.

DEDIU

According to Plato the human soul consists of three parts: the reason, the will and the desire. A man is happy when all three parts of the soul are in balance. Plato has thought about how to build a good society, and he proposed to transfer the leadership of a society to the wise.

THE SUN

Let's see some other quotations of Plato.

DEDIU

All things will be produced in superior quantity and quality, and with greater ease, when each man works at a single occupation, in accordance with his natural gifts, and at the right moment, without meddling with anything else.

Without effort, you cannot be prosperous. Though the land may be good, you cannot have an abundant crop without cultivation.

Better a little which is well done, than a great deal imperfectly.

For a man to conquer himself is the first and noblest of all victories.

I never did anything worth doing by accident, nor did any of my inventions come by accident; they came by work.

Necessity... the mother of invention.

The beginning is the most important part of the work.

It is a common saying, and in everybody's mouth, that life is but a sojourn.

And what, Socrates, is the food of the soul? Surely, I said, knowledge is the food of the soul.

For good nurture and education implant good constitutions.

If a man neglects education, he walks lame to the end of his life.

Ignorance, the root and stem of all evil.

Knowledge is true opinion.

Knowledge which is acquired under compulsion obtains no hold on the mind.

Let parents bequeath to their children not riches, but the spirit of reverence.

Music is the movement of sound to reach the soul for the education of its virtue.

No man should bring children into the world, who is unwilling to persevere to the end in their nature and education.

Opinion is the medium between knowledge and ignorance.

The direction in which education starts a man will determine his future in life.

The learning and knowledge that we have, is, at the most, but little compared with that of which we are ignorant.

There is no harm in repeating a good thing.

Twice and thrice over, as they say, good is it to repeat and review what is good.

We ought to esteem it of the greatest importance, that the fictions, which children first hear, should be adapted in the most perfect manner to the promotion of virtue.

To love rightly is to love what is orderly and beautiful in an educated and disciplined way.

Good people do not need laws to tell them to act responsibly, while bad people will find a way around the laws.

Injustice is censured because the censures are afraid of suffering, and not from any fear which they have of doing injustice.

Justice in the life and conduct of the State is possible only as first it resides in the hearts and souls of the citizens.

Justice means minding one's own business and not meddling with other men's concerns.

Man never legislates, but destinies and accidents, happening in all sorts of ways, legislate in all sorts of ways.

No law or ordinance is mightier than understanding.

Not to help justice in its need would be an impiety.

The highest reach of injustice is to be deemed just when you are not.

To go to the world below, having a soul which is like a vessel full of injustice, is the last and worst of all the evils.

When a Benefit is wrongly conferred, the author of the Benefit may often be said to injure.

All the gold which is under or upon the earth is not enough to give in exchange for virtue.

At the touch of love everyone becomes a poet.

Love is the joy of the good, the wonder of the wise, the amazement of the Gods.

Music is a moral law. It gives soul to the universe, wings to the mind, flight to the imagination, and charm and gaiety to life and to everything.

Poets utter great and wise things, which they do not themselves understand.

Then not only an old man, but also a drunkard, becomes a second time a child.

This City is what it is because our citizens are what they are.

Wise men speak because they have something to say; Fools because they have to say something.

Astronomy compels the soul to look upwards and leads us from this world to another.

We ought to fly away from earth to heaven as quickly as we can; and to fly away is to become like God, as far as this is possible; and to become like him is to become holy, just, and wise.

A state arises, as I conceive, out of the needs of mankind; no one is self-sufficing, but all of us have many wants.

Courage is knowing what not to fear.

Democracy passes into despotism.

Democracy... is a charming form of government, full of variety and disorder; and dispensing a sort of equality to equals and unequals alike.

Dictatorship naturally arises out of democracy, and the most aggravated form of tyranny and slavery out of the most extreme liberty.

Excess generally causes reaction, and produces a change in the opposite direction, whether it be in the seasons, or in individuals, or in governments.

Excess of liberty, whether it lies in state or individuals, seems only to pass into excess of slavery.

For the introduction of a new kind of music must be shunned as imperiling the whole state; since styles of music are never disturbed without affecting the most important political institutions.

Good actions give strength to ourselves and inspire good actions in others.

He who is not a good servant will not be a good master.

No one ever teaches well, who wants to teach, or governs well, who wants to govern.

One of the penalties for refusing to participate in politics is that you end up being governed by your inferiors.

Only the dead have seen the end of war.

Our object in the construction of the state is the greatest happiness of the whole, and not that of any one class.

Rhetoric is the art of ruling the minds of men.

States are as the men, they grow out of human characters.

The curse of me and my nation is that we always think things can be bettered by immediate action of some sort, any sort rather than no sort.

The measure of a man is what he does with power.

The most virtuous are those who content themselves with being virtuous without seeking to appear so.

The punishments which the wise suffer, who refuse to take part in the government, is to live under the government of worse men.

The rulers of the state are the only persons who ought to have the privilege of lying, either at home or abroad; they may be allowed to lie for the good of the state.

The wisest have the most authority.

There will be no end to the troubles of states, or of humanity itself, till philosophers become kings in this world, or till those we now call kings and rulers really and truly become philosophers, and political power and philosophy thus come into the same hands.

This and no other is the root from which a tyrant springs; when he first appears he is a protector.

We are twice armed if we fight with faith.

When the tyrant has disposed of foreign enemies by conquest or treaty, and there is nothing more to fear from them, then he is always stirring up some war or other, in order that the people may require a leader.

When there is an income tax, the just man will pay more and the unjust less on the same amount of income.

Attention to health is life's greatest hindrance.

THE SUN

Because Aristotle was the best student of Plato, let's see some of Aristotle's quotations.

DEDIU

It is the mark of an educated mind to rest satisfied with the degree of precision, which the nature of the subject admits, and not to seek exactness where only an approximation is possible.

Nature does nothing uselessly.

Teaching is the highest form of understanding.

The secret to humor is surprise.

The roots of education are bitter, but the fruit is sweet.

It is the mark of an educated mind to be able to entertain a thought without accepting it.

THE SUN
    Tell me about Vergilius.
DEDIU
    Exactly half a millennium after Pythagoras' birth, 357 years after Plato's birth, when Cicero was 36, and Caesar 30, in 70 BC, Publius Vergilius Maro was born in Andes, a town in the Roman province of Gallia Cisalpina (now Pietole Vecchia, a short distance from the center of Pietole, which is a part of Virgilio, a municipality in the Province of Mantova, in Lombardia, located about 130 km southeast of Milano, and about 6 km south of Mantova, in northern Italy), to a wealthy farming family.
When Vergilius was about 10 years old, his father took him to Cremona, about 60 km west of Andes, to begin his studies.
At 12 or 13 Vergilius' father moved him to Milano, about 75 km northwest of Cremona, to study there.
THE SUN
    When did he move to Roma (Rome)?
DEDIU
    When Vergilius was about 17 years old, his father moved him to Rome, to continue his studies in rhetoric, philosophy, and law.
Four years later, in 49 BC, Julius Caesar says *"**Alea iacta est**"* (The die is cast) and crosses the Rubicon (a shallow river in northeastern Italy, 250 km north of Rome, about 80 km long, running from the Apennine Mountains to the Adriatic Sea, between the towns of Cesena and Rimini), invading Italy. He seizes control of Rome. Soon after, Vergilius, 21, moves to Napoli (Naples) and studies with Greek (perhaps Epicurean (Epicurus, 341 BC – 269 BC)) scholars there.
THE SUN
    When did Vergilius begin to write?
DEDIU
    At the age of 25 Vergilius begins to work on the *Eclogues.* One year later, on March 15, 44 BC, Julius Caesar was killed. Then a civil war breaks out, and Octavian, who was 7 years younger than Vergilius, eventually emerges as the winner. Octavian's mother Aita was a niece of Julius Caesar, who adopted him as his heir (Aita was the daughter of Julia, sister to Julius Caesar). Octavian was consul

in 43 BC (at 20), 33 BC, and 31 – 23 BC. In 27 BC, at 36, he became emperor, and in 23 BC, at 40, he receives extended powers, adds the name Augustus, the Roman Republic ends, and the Roman Empire starts.

THE SUN

Very good. More details are presented in the first part of this book.

DEDIU

Right. Now let's see more quotations.

Publius Vergilius Maro
70 BC – 19 BC
Roman poet

Felix, qui potuit rerum cognoscere causas - Fortunate is he, who understood the causes of things.

Fervet opus - The work boils.

Facilis descensus Averno - The descent to hell is easy.

Famam extendere factis - To extend his fame by deeds.

Mens agitat molem – Mind drives matter

Varium et mutabile semper femina – Woman is always a changeable and capricious thing.

O passi gravoria, dabit deus his quoque finem – Oh, suffering ones, God will grant an end to these things too.

Possunt quia posse videntur - They can because they think they can.

Adeo in teneris consuescere multum est - It is imperative to be well trained in early youth.

Ab uno disce omnes - From one example, learn all.

Ad utrumque paratus - Ready for both; prepared for either alternative.

Durate et vosmet rebus servate secundis - Carry on and preserve yourselves for better times.

Amor vincit omnia - Love conquers all.

Agnosco veteris vestigia flammae - I recognize the signs of the old flame.

Aeternum servans sub pectore vulnus - Nursing an everlasting wound within the breast.

The Ammonoosuc River running south towards back, with part of the southeast side of the Mount Washington Resort (1902, right).

Quintus Horatius Flaccus
65 BC – 8 BC
Roman lyric poet

Carpe diem - Enjoy the present day

Facile largire de alieno - It is easy to be generous with things of another person

Fallentis semitia vitae - The narrow path of a private life

Fari quae sentiat - To say what one feels

Nothing is beautiful from every point of view.

Coram populo - In the presence of the public

Often you must turn your stylus to erase, if you hope to write anything worth a second reading.

Integer vitae - Honest life

Callida iunctura - Skillful joining, careful workmanship

He will always be a slave who does not know how to live upon a little.

Faenum habet in cornu, longe fuge - He has hay on his horn, keep your distance (reference to a charging bull)

Caelum non animum mutant qui mare currunt - Sky, not souls, do they change, those who cross the sea.

Eheu! fugaces labuntur anni – Alas! The fleeting years are passing.

Sedit qui timuit ne non succederet – He, who feared he would not succeed, sat still.

In pace, ut sapiens, aptarit idonea bello - In peace, as a wise man, he appropriately prepares for war.

A picture is a poem without words.

Words will not fail when the matter is well considered.

Remember, when life's path is steep, to keep your mind even.

Si quid novisti rectius istis, candidus imperti; si nil, his utere mecum - If you can better these principles, tell me; if not, join me in following them.

Begin, be bold and venture to be wise.

Choose a subject equal to your abilities; think carefully what your shoulders may refuse, and what they are capable of bearing.

Ab ovo usque ad mala - From the egg to the apples (from the beginning to the end).

Clogged with yesterday's excess, the body drags the mind down with it.

Cease to inquire what the future has in store, and take as a gift whatever the day brings forth.

Ad unguem factus homo -A man accomplished to his fingertips (a fully accomplished man).

A word once uttered can never be recalled.

Dimidium facti, qui coepit habet - He who has begun is half done.

Culpam poena premit comes - Punishment follows closely behind crime's heels.

Fidelity is the sister of justice.

One wanders to the left, another to the right. Both are equally in error, but, are seduced by different delusions.

Naturam expellas furca, tamen usque recurret - Nature can be expelled with a fork, but nevertheless always returns.

Aequam servare mentem - To preserve a calm mind; equanimity.

Aequam memento rebus in arduis servare mentem - Remember to maintain a calm mind while doing difficult tasks.

Anger is a short madness.

Subdue your passion or it will subdue you.

From the bridge over the Ammonoosuc River, the east side of the Mount Washington Resort (1902, elevation 500 m).

Publius Ovidius Naso
43 BC - 17 AD
Roman poet

Candor dat viribus alas - Candor gives wings to strength

Fas est et ab hoste doceri - It is right to learn even from an enemy

Candida pax - Candid peace

Candida me capiet, capiet me flava puella - The blonde will charm me, the brunette will charm me too.

Perfer et obdura; dolor hic tibi proderit olim - Be patient and tough; someday this pain will be useful to you.

Omnia mutantur, nihil interit - All things change, nothing perishes.

My hopes are not always realized, but I always hope.

The man who has experienced shipwreck, shudders even at a calm sea.

The sharp thorn often produces delicate roses.

A horse never runs so fast as when he has other horses to catch up and outpace.

The will is commendable, though the ability may be wanting.

Courage conquers all things: it even gives strength to the body.

The burden which is well borne becomes light.

Venus favors the bold.

Neither can the wave that has passed by be recalled, nor the hour which has passed return again.

Everything comes gradually and at its appointed hour.

Time is the devourer of all things.

Time, motion and wine cause sleep.

At times it is folly to hasten, at other times, to delay. The wise do everything in its proper time.

Use the occasion, for it passes swiftly.

You can learn from anyone, even your enemy.

Abeunt studia in mores - Studies change into habits.

Adde parvum parvo magnus acervus erit - Add a little to a little and there will be a great heap

If you want to be loved, be lovable.

Alas! How difficult it is not to betray one's guilt by one's looks.

The penalty may be removed, the crime is eternal.

What is deservedly suffered must be borne with calmness, but when the pain is unmerited, the grief is resistless.

Happy is the man who has broken the chains which hurt the mind, and has given up worrying once and for all.

Everyone's a millionaire where promises are concerned.

Beauty is a fragile gift.

In our leisure we reveal what kind of people we are.

The lamp burns bright when wick and oil are clean.

What is it that love does to a woman? Without, she only sleeps; with it alone, she lives.

Whether they give or refuse, it delights women just the same to have been asked.

Why should I go into details, we have nothing that is not perishable except what our hearts and our intellects endows us with.

Daring is not safe against daring men.

Fortune and love favor the brave.

Happy are those who dare courageously to defend what they love.

Men do not value a good deed unless it brings a reward.

A prince should be slow to punish, and quick to reward.

People are slow to claim confidence in undertakings of magnitude.

Tears at times have the weight of speech.

The heavier crop is ever in others' fields.

Like fragile ice, anger passes away in time.

Ah me! Love cannot be cured by herbs.

There is more refreshment and stimulation in a nap, even of the briefest, than in all the alcohol ever distilled.

There is no such thing as pure pleasure; some anxiety always goes with it.

Time is generally the best doctor.

Suppressed grief suffocates, it rages within the breast, and is forced to multiply its strength.

Take rest; a field that has rested gives a beautiful crop.

The cause is hidden; the effect is visible to all.

To feel our ills is one thing, but to cure them is another.

What is without periods of rest will not endure.

The Gold Room in the Mount Washington Resort, where the documents of the United Nations Monetary and Financial Conference were signed in July 1944.

Tiberius Julius Caesar Augustus
42 BC – 37 AD
Second Roman Emperor from 14 AD to 37 AD

Power has no limits.

It is the duty of a good shepherd to shear his sheep, not to skin them.

To have command is to have all the power you will ever need. To have all the power you will ever need, is to have the world in the palm of your hand.

Let them hate me, provided they respect my conduct.

The fireplace on the first floor of the Mount Washington Resort (1902, by Joseph Stickney (1840 – 1903, coal business)).

Lucius Annaeus Seneca
4 BC - 65 AD
Roman Stoic philosopher, statesman and dramatist

Our plans miscarry because they have no aim. When a man does not know what harbor he is making for, no wind is the right wind.

Let us train our minds to desire what the situation demands.

To govern is to serve, not to rule.

Timendi causa est nescire - The cause of fear is ignorance.

Ad nocendum patentes sumus - We all have power to do harm.

Fallaces sunt rerum species et hominum spes fallunt - The appearances of things are deceptive and the hope of men is deceived

Non est ad astra mollis e terris via - There is no easy way from the Earth to the stars.

Si vis amari, ama - If you want to be loved, love.

Homines dum docent discunt - Men learn while they teach

It is a rough road that leads to the heights of greatness.

Dante Alighieri
1265 – 1321
Italian Florentine poet

Lasciate ogne speranza, voi ch'entrate. - All hope abandon, ye who enter in.

Necessità 'l ci 'nduce, e non diletto. - Necessity brings him here, not pleasure.

Bene ascolta chi la nota. - He listens well who takes notes.

La dimanda onesta
si de' seguir con l'opera tacendo.
A fair request should be followed by the deed in silence.

Libertà va cercando, ch'è sì cara,
come sa chi per lei vita rifiuta.
He goes seeking liberty, which is so dear, as he knows who for it renounces life.

Puro e disposto a salire a le stelle. - Pure and disposed to mount unto the stars.

L'esperîenza
di questa dolce vita.
The experience of this sweet life.

L'amor che muove il sole e l'altre stelle. - The Love which moves the Sun and the other stars.

William Shakespeare
1564 – 1616
English poet and playwright

Love all, trust a few, do wrong to none.

We know what we are, but know not what we may be.

All the world's a stage, and all the men and women merely players: they have their exits and their entrances; and one man in his time plays many parts, his acts being seven ages.

Women may fall when there's no strength in men.

Be not afraid of greatness: some are born great, some achieve greatness, and some have greatness thrust upon them.

Better three hours too soon than a minute too late.
Brevity is the soul of wit.

The east side of the Highland Lighthouse, at 27 Highland Light Rd, North Truro, 10 km east of Provincetown, northeast of Cape Cod.

John Milton
1608 – 1674
English poet and author

The mind is its own place, and in itself, can make heaven of Hell, and a hell of Heaven.

A good book is the precious lifeblood of a master spirit.

Give me the liberty to know, to utter, and to argue freely according to conscience, above all liberties.

He who reigns within himself and rules passions, desires, and fears is more than a king.

Love-quarrels oft in pleasing concord end.

None can love freedom heartily, but good men; the rest love not freedom, but license.

The superior man acquaints himself with many sayings of antiquity, and many deeds of the past, in order to strengthen his character thereby.

Blaise Pascal
1623 – 1662
French mathematician, physicist, philosopher and writer

It is not certain that everything is uncertain.

Since we cannot know all that there is to be known about anything, we ought to know a little about everything.

Love has reasons which reason cannot understand.

The heart has its reasons that the mind knows nothing of.

The Pilgrims Monument in the center of Provincetown, built with granite between 1907 and 1910, commemorates the first landfall of the Pilgrims in 1620, and the signing in Provincetown Harbor of the Mayflower Compact.

THE SUN
    Very good, Dediu. I like very much your quote

The most important thing on Earth is The Sun.

    You are absolutely right! Now I would like to see some of your other quotes.

Michael M. Dediu
1943 –
American philosopher, mathematician, writer

Your footprints on the sands of time are made by your running creativity and hard work.

It is very important and difficult to improve the world, but even more important and much more difficult is to improve ourselves.

All the great things have been said long ago, but we don't learn them, and for this we continue to repeat the same mistakes generation after generation.

Grateful children, beautiful old ladies and good neighbors cannot be found.

The mediocretization of the society is progressing dangerously fast.

How many years are in your life matters, but how much life is in your years really makes your mark.

The money doesn't matter, only its number.

It is a rara avis (rare bird), but if you are fortunate enough to find somebody who is better than you and wants to help, open your heart.

Loving is the highest form of living.

There is imperfection in everything, the question is how much.

Everybody can have bad ideas; the challenge is to create good ideas.

When there is progress in some areas, the people must work very hard not to have regress in some other areas.

The progress of a society is determined by science and technology.

The Sun is much more vital than we think, and it has many more millions of surprises.

The Sun is a necessary condition for life on Earth, but not sufficient.

The time and space are infinite, and a new mathematical proof was given: particles charged in a magnetic field can escape into infinity without ever stopping.

Don't get nervous because of a bad man or a bad car: just give them to somebody who can repair them.

For good health: buy healthy foods, cook them properly, and eat them abstemiously.

The roots of many diseases essentially are in the genes.

Negative thinking is permanent; positive thinking is a rara avis (rare bird), and is very healthy.

To get healthier we need mathematics, because complex biological structures and healing processes can be better comprehended only by using advanced mathematics.

Solutions for many problems can be found with mathematical analysis and medical help.

All the bad things done by people have a medical explanation.

The bad people need medical help, not prison. From prisons they usually come out worse. From specialized hospitals, there is a chance to cure them, and then they will pay the bill for treatment.

Your age is important, but more important is your life expectancy.

Achievement is not permanent success, but how fast you recover from a fiasco.

Success, defined at the highest international level, will not lower its standard to you; you need to elevate your standard to success.

Much can be learned from accomplishments, but even more from fiascos.

Good achievers know to divide difficult projects in manageable small tasks.

Always the mediocrities, and their banalities, dominate. Always!

If you notice that you go in a wrong direction, the sooner you turn back, the better.

If you work hard, in a good direction, with a clear and useful objective, the success will suddenly find you.

It is great to create a new product, even greater if it is well tested.

If you categorically want to do a good task, that's passion, not work.

The more passion you have, the greater achiever you'll be.

Mature and proven leaders are always better.

Logic and imagination go hand in hand for great achievers.

Those who want to have great achievements don't schedule meetings, they work.

To be creative, do not follow others on their paths; create instead your own path.

For achievement one needs a good direction, hard work, persistence, tenacity, and the will to never give up.

When you have many tasks in front of you, start with the hardest one, the others will smoothly follow.

Some failures and errors are inevitable; use them to learn and improve.

The best defense on the ground is a strong space and air offensive force.

Good achievers need reliable feedback from their teams; for this they cultivate an atmosphere of trust and collaboration.

It is good to offer the people what they want, but it is much better to offer them something better.

Best leaders and achievers know how to release the energy and talent of their teams.

Ad praesens amet qui nunquam amavit; quique amavit, ad praesens amet - May he love today who has never loved before; and may he who has loved, love today as well.

The loudness and aggressiveness are invers proportional to the intelligence and reason.

To discern between good and bad, in complex situations, one needs common sense, knowledge, intelligence and experience.

Your contacts and friends describe you.

Arrogance and self-importance are everywhere, modesty is a rara avis (rare bird).

In life try to help yourself, your family, your friends and others. When you cannot help much, just do not create problems.

To have security, eliminate the threats.

It is very easy to be pessimist; choose the difficult one, and be optimist.

Loyalty comes from intense liking and appreciation.

Money is a part of happiness, but not the most important.

Common sense is essential for success, and education helps.

New skills encourage success.

A strong family, with father, mother and their children, is the foundation of any good country. Without this foundation, any country will disappear.

One way to achieve success is to do what you like, you know well and it is useful for many people.

To be successful, you need to sell.

Triumph causes self-righteousness.
Self-righteousness causes laziness.
Laziness causes fiasco.

Time is so precious and so little; you never know when it's gone.

Few people know,
How much you have to know,
To know,
How little you know.

Be hungrier for knowledge than for food.

Even a drop of education can change the color of an ocean of ignorance.

Computers are tools for education, not substitutes of it.

If we are over 30, we should ask not what our parents can do for us, but what we can do for our parents.

Many laws are made by those who temporarily are in power, to impose their immoral views on the great majority of moral people, but, of course, in the end, the moral people always win.

Happiness comes when you do good things for you, your family, your friends and many others.

Creativity comes from observation, knowledge and thinking at square.

Innovation is applied creativity.

Mathematical algorithms and camera technology will make better global positioning systems (GPS).

In capitalism everybody complains that men exploit men. In communism and socialism is vice-versa of men exploit men, but everybody applauds, when directed.

Television was created by scientists and engineers to be a tool for learning and good entertainment, but the politicians and their friends use it for bad propaganda.

Life and death are interrelated, they cannot exist without each other, but the life should have much more time to be around, and here the medical assistance is vital.

Science and technology are the engines of progress.

The Internet is like a huge library – keep it clean and unpolluted.
The space and time are infinite.

USA, Massachusetts, Cape Cod, the northeast part of Provincetown Inn (back left), green grass on 13 Dec. 2015, looking west.